SHIFT
HAPPENS

How I Won a Million Dollars
with the Law of Attraction

A Step-by-Step Guide
to Manifesting Your Dreams

Candi Parker

ParkerHouseBooks.com

Liability Disclaimer

This book is lovingly dedicated to my brothers

Jimmy and Steve Parker,

Who have re-emerged into pure positive energy.

They always believed in me.

I wish to express my heartfelt gratitude to the following people who have helped to make this book possible:

Nancy Matthews, my amazing and brilliant coach, Judee Light, my awesome editor, and Tom Parker, Nancy Roth and Kathie Reeves for their love and support throughout this process.

All of you have been there with me every step of the way and you have filled the journey with love, laughter, wisdom and joy.

TABLE OF CONTENTS

INTRODUCTION

What you're about to discover is one of the secrets to living a happy, positive life. It's about a universal law that so few really understand. When I had my own personal experience with it, my life changed forever; and not because of the material things I received, which of course are wonderful, but because I learned how to apply this universal law in every area of my life.

There are many 'universal laws' in our existence such as Newton's discovery of the law of gravity, Einstein's law of relativity, the law of cause and effect, etc. The Encyclopedia Britannica states: "a law is universal if it states that some conditions, so far as are known, invariably are found together with certain other conditions...."

The universal laws are always working whether or not we believe them or understand them. They are based on the quantum knowledge that everything is energy; and everything in the universe, including us, is connected through this energy. What we feel, think, say and do are all forms of energy through which our realities are created. This book is about one of those universal laws, the Law of Attraction, and how I utilized it to go from being a poverty stricken widow to having a million dollars.

It happened to me and it can happen to you! It doesn't take genius to understand the Law of Attraction. Special talents are not needed. You don't need to be lucky or privileged. However, you do have to make your vibration a priority in your life and be willing to focus the time and energy on doing what it takes to create the life you really want. You must be willing to shift your thinking and think good thoughts. It may seem challenging to believe that just thinking good thoughts can change your life, but trust me, it has a profound impact on your reality and the way you think about yourself, your job, your relationships, your health and your wealth.

I know part of the reason that you picked up this book is because you want to know how you can have a million dollars, too, and I'm here to tell you that you absolutely can. It may not happen today, it may not happen tomorrow, but I promise you that if you follow the instructions outlined in this book and practice them with consistency the same way that I did, whatever you want can be created and manifested in your life. Yes, I got a million dollars, and I also got other things I wanted, a beautiful smile, fencing my acreage, horses, renovating my house, travel to beautiful places. In this book I share the details on how I specifically manifested those things, and what is most important is the foundation that I laid to create those results. In Chapter Four when we get to the actual event of my receiving the million dollars, you see how I actually created it with the changes in my thoughts and my vibration.

You have your dreams. You have different wants and desires than mine. This book shows you how to manifest what you want, because life is about your personal design, the personal tapestry that you are creating.

Please take your time with this book. Absorb the ideas, practice the principles, the suggestions and exercises in here and watch the life of your dreams begin to unfold.

These are the things that I did.

There are no coincidences.

This book is in your hands for a reason.

4

CHAPTER ONE

"Thoughts become things."
~ Mike Dooley

CREATE A NEW REALITY

So what, exactly, is the Law of Attraction?

Basically it is this: you attract into your life circumstances that are the same or similar to those you are focusing on. Your energy always matches with similar energy. Your thoughts have vibrational energy patterns that resonate with similar circumstances that match your attitudes and beliefs. You attract people to you that match what you believe.

The Law of Attraction is the way that we manifest our reality. Simply put, you can only attract what is in harmony with you. And once you really understand the Law of Attraction, you can apply it consciously and change your life immediately, re-creating your life to manifest your dreams. You can become more prosperous in every area of your life.

Today there are many teachers of the art of using this Law, and there are many books and DVDs about the Law of Attraction. It is my goal to take what I have learned from them, having successfully applied in my life, and present it to you in a way that sparks new ideas, rekindles old dreams and gives you a step-by-step way to manifest them, with personal stories for demonstration...leading up to the day I was surprised to receive a million dollars. Yes, we can consciously direct our vibrations. You can intentionally and easily create a joyful life. Begin now! It really is all about how you think! Are your thoughts consistently positive, wealthy, happy thoughts?

It is true that what you think about comes about - both positively and negatively. We all have the ability to use our thoughts to dictate the vibration we are in and the life we creating. What are you creating today? Take a moment to look at your life as you are living it right now. Be as honest as you can. Are you at peace? Do you love your life?

What you think about all day long is what you believe to be true. What you affirm with your thoughts is what you are bringing about in your life. For example, "I'll never get ahead." "My back is killing me." "It's driving me crazy." "There's never enough." "I can't have that." "I can't stand that." "I'll never be able to afford that." "I'm overwhelmed." "I don't have this." "I'll never have that."

Life doesn't just happen to you, it is created by what you think and say! If your thoughts are continually focused on

6

what you don't have, then the more you notice the things that you don't have because that is what you are focusing on.

This present moment is all you have.

Right now. And right now you have the ability to change your life! Here it is again:

- What you think about is what you are actually affirming for your life.

- What you affirm with your thoughts is what you bring about in your life.

- Life doesn't just happen to you, it is created by what you think and say!

You may want to stop and think about how powerful that is and the responsibility and power it gives you! Pay attention to the words that come out of your mouth; they are expressions of your thinking. What do you chatter about all day? Really listen to what you say and how you say it.

Once again, they are expressions of what you are thinking! You may be unaware that that you are thinking a less than positive thought, that's how unconscious it may be. Perhaps you may worry about paying bills, or stress about getting everything done that you are supposed to. These kinds of thoughts just bring more of your attention to them and keep you in a less than positive vibration. This is a good time to remember that what you give your thoughts and energy to is manifesting. What can you shift to and put your focus on that is positive? What makes you feel glad? Shift your focus to that. It raises your vibration and you attract positive results even on the things you were worrying and stressing over. One shift at a time.

Less than positive people believe that the worst is going to happen. People who think in a negative way have their beliefs reinforced by a media machine that tends to focus on what is not working in the world. You carry with you those images they show you, if not consciously then unconsciously. Why keep those thoughts in your head? Why imprint yourself that way?

Less than positive people talk all day long about all of the negative things going on in their lives and in the world. As their day goes, they seek out people who listen and agree with them — because that is a way that they signal to themselves and others that they are right. Positive thinking people are committed to noticing and shifting their thoughts and avoiding that trap. They understand that improving how they feel means clearing from their lives negative people and situations and increasing their positive thinking.

To that end, they do not watch the news or violence; because they know putting their attention on those things make them feel less positive. They take pleasure from life and think about all of the things they are grateful for.

Positive people grow happier and more positive each

day, because that is what they are focusing on.

One of the most important lessons I've learned is this:

**To become more positive, you have to
BE more positive.**

How do you do that? To become more positive you have to be more positive? How can you BE more positive? You can start by doing things and saying things that positive people would do and say. Start acting as if it is so and that things are as you want them. Look for people in your life or online that you can model. What do they say and do that makes you recognize them as positive people?

To be more positive you have to look at life differently. This may seem too obvious to mention, but it came as a bit of a surprise to me. Many of us got to know about life by doing work we don't love. We may have learned, and accepted as fact, that life is hard, dull and boring. And perhaps that belief is deep in the core of who we are. With that idea in mind, it's no wonder we look for promises of quick fixes and easy money. I don't think they exist. I've tried them, haven't you?

To create a healthy and a wealthy attitude, you need to put yourself in the vibration of thriving and add to that vibration by exercising a valuable skill: Consciously changing your thoughts, because 'thoughts become things.' It may seem less than easy at first, because of old habits. It may take you time to get good at it - you keep getting better

9

as you do it! That's one of the reasons I believe, as my teachers do, that the most important thing you can do to regain your health is to think positive thoughts. And to acquire wealth you must think wealthy thoughts. Look at it this way: it gives you a tremendous advantage in life and pays off in just about every area of your life. As you practice living a more positive, more joyful life, you accelerate your happiness and your health and your wealth.

As with anything, the more you practice, the better you get. By "thinking healthy and wealthy" I mean that you have the ability to look at any situation and decide how you can look at it differently and in a more positive, healthy way. Consciously choosing to put the positive spin on it, even if you don't want to, is the practice of healthy and wealthy thinking. If you can figure out how to be positive when everybody else is throwing their hands up, you'll be prosperous and happy sooner than you even think you can be. Also, if you apply this thinking to your business, you can figure out solutions before your colleagues. A positive mental attitude is achieved by training your mind to think and believe in a hopeful and productive manner about yourself and others.

In **Part 2 - the Workbook**, you will find exercises to assist you in creating a positive life. Let's start developing your skills now with a thought provoking exercise. Here is the exercise:

Spend a few minutes today thinking about:

- how to think positively

- how to look at things differently and

- how to communicate from this place of positivity

Here are some ideas. Perhaps you can catch yourself when you are thinking less than positive thoughts and think of how to reframe them. Think of a situation that you consider less than positive and about how you can look at that situation more positively. Think about how you can respond positively to someone who speaks negatively to you. Use a worksheet to expand on your thoughts and list the things you come up with.

Next, think about ways you can be more positive. It may be that you look for people to model, or place positive quotes around you, in your environment or on your computer, and smile at everyone you meet today...you maybe surprised at how many ideas you can come up with. Make a nice long list. Also, go to your Facebook page and tell everyone, including me, "Today I am..." State your intentions and you'll be more likely to stay aware of them and do them. For instance, "Today I am looking for the good in everything."

As with anything, when you practice you become more skilled at it. You may use this skill to increase your income, too! It's easier than you think. Make another list on how you can improve your ability to create money in your life.

Here's an idea to get you started. Make a list of things you can sell that you are ready to part with or no longer use. Post them on Craigslist.org or Ebay.com or have a good old-fashioned yard sale. Better yet, involve the whole neighborhood! Set a day for everyone to have a yard sale and advertise for free on Craigslist.org or other community boards or newspapers.

What other ways can you think of to create money? Do you have a recipe you can work with? How about that idea for an invention you secretly harbor? Or perhaps a service that you can offer? What are you good at? Ask yourself, "I wonder what else is possible?" and watch lots of ideas bubble up for you to look at. Allow all ideas to flow as they can lead to more and more ideas. If this is not easy for you then carry the list with you all day and when you have inspired thought write it down. Set a goal for yourself to write down ten ways to create money.

Get into the habit of practicing being positive daily. This may show you exactly how you've been thinking... and you may realize what being less than positive has been doing to you and what your life becomes if you stay on that track. Make yourself a promise, like I did. I promised myself that I would do whatever it took to make sure that each day was better than the one before. I made a commitment to myself to think happier, healthier and wealthier thoughts every day. That may seem like a simple promise, but it had a profound impact on the way I thought about myself including my work, my relationships and making money. It made me see that many of my thoughts were not healthy. It also gave me the motivation I needed to shift my thinking, to start something new, to think differently than I had been. This little technique is simple and easy to apply. Simple changes can lead to big results. This makes a positive difference. For example, if you are someone who wants to lose weight and you continually drink sodas, then having one less soda per week results in a loss of calories and pounds. And, just one less soda a day has even faster results. What is one simple thing that you can do towards your goal or towards having a better life?

For each day to be better than the last you have to focus on that happening. You have to "see" it, believe it can happen, act as if it were already so, and be grateful that it is the way things are. Can you feel the shift in vibrations in that last sentence? A grateful vibration acts like a magic magnet, drawing to you the things you are already grateful for having.

Being grateful for having something in advance of its appearing is the key!

Happy people are happy thinkers. Choose thoughts that keep you focused on positive outcomes and give you a feeling of happiness. So, how do you do that? For people who want to shift their thinking here's an easy way to start: The first thing to do is catch yourself saying negative words or thinking negative thoughts. Now that you have recognized it, you can acknowledge your amazing thought control and then find the reverse of that thought or word and say it to yourself a few times. If you just practice this one technique as often as you can it becomes easier and easier and you soon recognize a shift within your thinking.

The most important thing to remember is that you have to do the work to stay positive; no one can do it for you. Place yourself in environments that foster these feelings. Surround yourself with people and events that resonate with your positive thinking. Start now. Now is always the best time to start something good. Why wait a moment longer to start living a more positive life or do something good for yourself? Create your life as you want it to be. The sooner you begin, the faster you'll be living it. Read on and discover more tools and techniques that I used and take whatever information works for you and implement it now.

"Yesterday is gone and its tale told.
Today new seeds are growing."
~ Rumi

Think of a time when you wished you had done something sooner. Well, you can do something else now, and the sooner you start then the sooner it arrives. You have in your hands the tools to create whatever you want. As you clean up your thinking and realize that you can hold positive thoughts in the midst of a negative world, you notice that things within and around you start to shift. If the less than positive people around you do not get your supportive attention to the trials and tribulations of their lives then they go elsewhere to find it and you are free to focus on the positive things that feel good. You also attract like-minded thinkers into your sphere and when positive people align with each other they create an even bigger atmosphere of positivity.

You may find yourself feeling happier and smiling more. I was recently at a conference where I was feeling happy and was smiling all of the time. On several occasions I was on an elevator with hotel guests and had interesting encounters. At first each was in their own thoughts and world until I smiled at them. They smiled back at me. One man asked me why I was so happy; another person said I looked so positive, etc. What a wonderful opportunity to spread a positive vibration by smiling and talking to these people. In less than a minute people were shifted. Now, you can consciously participate in creating a new life with an attitude of joy and expectation, because you create your experiences by what you think and the new actions that you take!

**Understanding the Law of Attraction gives
you the knowing to consciously create
and manifest your own desires.**

Your thoughts determine what you focus on. So that means if you change your thoughts you change your life as you know it. Instead of thinking about your circumstances as they are, think about how you want them to be! This is enormously exciting! Your happiness and success are important to the world. In this book are the steps to creating what you really want. I did it and if I can do it, you can do it, too. Here's more on how:

Begin by visualizing yourself as happy and successful and loving what you do and start getting very clear on what you want.

What you dream of having while believing it to be so, manifests. I dreamed of being a millionaire and, because I gave it a lot of attention, I believe that my life became rearranged for it to happen. And the money allowed me to have the things I wanted. I made a decision to be more aware and conscious of my life, reminding myself daily to pay attention to the things I said and did, and then made choices about what I wanted.

Many times in my life when I wanted something, I would concentrate on it with gratitude, and it would show up. After my amazement faded, I would not remember that I had been concentrating on it because I would move on! Eventually I would visualize my desire for something else and it, too, would appear. You would think that having these experiences would keep me very excited to do more. But, I would not remember! Again.

The thing is, I was manifesting even when I was not concentrating on it, even when I would not remember. I was always manifesting. Because, when I was not concentrating on what I wanted, I was using my emotions and feelings to attract and manifest anyway. Was it what I really wanted? Was I aware that I was manifesting? No. Like many people I just thought life was "happening" to me. If you had looked at my life the way it was outside of my head at that time, you probably would have judged me, shaken your head and walked away. I began to live from inside my head. I made a list of the things that I would do with the money that I wanted to manifest. Hesitant at first to actually say a million dollars, I had to practice. I practiced saying it over and over, and it became easier and easier. Bob Proctor tells us to fill in the blank after, **"I'm so happy and grateful now that..."** which is my very best tool.

I immediately turned this phrase into a sign and posted it on my mirrors and doorways, and every time I saw my sign, I would fill in the blank with my desires, including a million dollars. Surrounding myself with reminders and taking seminars from millionaires and billionaires, I wanted to learn it all...from the ones who were already modeling the life that I wanted to have. I would "practice" being a millionaire in small ways. I went to the nearest yacht club and had lunch. I went to the French restaurant and ordered a glass of wine and a crème brûlé. You may laugh at these silly things that I was doing, however, they anchored my thinking about living a richer life. How many "silly" things can you think up to anchor your heart's desire? For instance, if you want a horse, go to horse shows, even volunteer. Help at a horse rescue. Get to know horse people. Visit a tack shop. How does one care for a horse? If you want a boat, visit a big tackle store, roam around and daydream. What kind of shoes do you wear on your boat? What kind of accoutrements does your boat need? Where is the nearest boat show? Or boat yard? Hang out at the docks. Talk to people. Make friends with people with boats. Think! What can you do to "play" with your dreams? Make up that silly list. It is a first step towards understanding what it feels like to already have your heart's desire.

Despite any appearance of not having enough, I would daydream and in my daydreams I would "feel" like a millionaire. And since it was a "feeling" that creates vibration I knew that I had to change my vibration before the money could come. So I concentrated on what it would "feel" like. Did you get that?

I had to change my vibration before the money could come!

It was my intention to raise my vibration to attract a million dollars, then I would be in a better position for it to happen and it would be easier to create it, as all things are better with practice. Build your dream muscle.

I am proof that ordinary people can accomplish extraordinary things if they just put the right things into their minds.

I listened.

I learned.

I did it!

So can you!

"Your real work is to decide what you want and then to focus upon it. For it is through focusing upon what you want that you will attract it. That is the process of creating"
~ Abraham-Hicks

Your imagination creates your future reality.

Remember when you were a kid and anything was possible? As kids, we imagine anything we want. We might tangle with pretend dragons, have an imaginary friend or be a fairy tale princess. Pretend play helps to develop new skills. Your imagination helps you to practice and apply your new learning and better understand how these new skills are used in the real world. Your imagination helps you become a creative thinker. As the oldest of eight children, I would lead my younger siblings in made-up games like "school" and "carnivals" and "parades". We had great parades. What kind of made up games did you play as a child? They came from your imagination.

Your imagination is so powerful! It is powerful enough to cause physiological reactions.

Let me demonstrate.

Think of a lemon, think of scratching the skin, and imagine the aroma of the lemon.

Imagine cutting the lemon open, smelling the wonderful lemony smell.

Imagine cutting a wedge off of the lemon, picking it up and bringing it up to your mouth. Now imagine taking a bite into the wedge of lemon.

Did you have a reaction in your mouth like producing excess saliva or a pucker? That simple exercise demonstrates the power of your mind. You didn't actually bite a lemon, you just thought it!

Imagine what happens when you consciously focus your thoughts on your dreams!

What is the truth?

Are you enduring life . . . or creating it?

What would you like the truth to be?

Give yourself permission to dream big.

Let your imagination run wild! Now, before you start the dream exercises in Chapter 2, take a moment to sit quietly and get yourself in the vibration to dream. Whatever you want to attract to you, you must have thoughts and feelings that match it. Then it appears easily. It may seem like magic and then you realize what it really is: perseverance, diligence and a belief that what you want is already so.

"Imagination is more important than knowledge."
~Albert Einstein

Chapter One Summary

- You attract into your life circumstances that are the same or similar to what you are focusing on.

- You can only attract what is in harmony with you.

- What you think about comes about - both positively and negatively

- Life is created by what we think and say!

- Positive people are committed to noticing and shifting their thoughts

- Get into the habit of practicing being positive daily.

- Being grateful for having something in advance of it appearing is key!

- Catch yourself saying negative words or thinking negative thoughts, then find the reverse of that thought or word and say it to yourself a few times.

- Instead of thinking about your circumstances as they are, think about how you want them to be!

- What you dream of having while believing it to be so, manifests.

"At the center of your being you have the answer;
you know who you are and you know what you want."
~ Lao Tzu

CHAPTER TWO

STEPS

Follow these simple steps and create the life that you dream of...

- Choose.
- See.
- Believe.
- Feel.
- Thanks.

"The greatest reward in becoming a millionaire is not the amount of money that you earn. It is the kind of person that you have to become to become a millionaire in the first place." ~ Jim Rohn

I allow my income to constantly expand and I live in comfort and joy!

What you radiate outward in your thoughts, feelings, mental pictures and words, you attract into your life.

~ Catherine Ponder

ONE: CHOOSE...

Decide what it is you really want.

Let me ask you something...would you call up a catalog store and say, "Oh, just send me anything in the catalog"? Of course not! You would put your order in. You would say, "This is what I want." And once you gave your order, you would believe that it was being sent to you. Would you keep putting the same order in over and over? No! You know that it is on the way to you. You expect it.

So... What is your order? What would you like? What would fill your heart with joy and your soul with contentment? What are your heart's desires? Take a moment to consider your possibilities. The only limits you have are in your mind. You have more possibilities than you can act on. Look at things as they can be. Imagine your possibilities and your vision expands! You are putting an order out into the Universe.

"The mind moves in the direction of our currently dominant thoughts". ~ Earl Nightingale

Now make a list of those desires. Come from your heart. Put everything on your list that you feel you need and everything that you want. What do you really want? Be honest with yourself.

This list is the first step to manifesting what you really want. It is very personal so I suggest that you share your

27

list only with those people you know support you to keep your energy strong and pure, and your own thinking clear and certain. It is easy to feel less than confident when someone else gives you their opinion on your choices. Remember to keep your lips zipped to people in general. Some people may tell you that they don't think what you are doing is going to work, or say something to deny the truth of what you are saying and dreaming of having or doing. Now, they probably don't mean any harm. Most likely they are just projecting their own refusal to believe upon you. This can have an effect on you, though, causing doubt and insecurity. It happened to me. I was at a business retreat one time where I was asked what my dream or goal for my personal future was. It was a defining moment for me as I struggled with announcing my deepest desire to others. I was internally deciding if this was a 'safe' place to mention my most private heart's desire and everything I had been imagining and practicing.

I had recently returned from T. Harv Eker's Millionaire Mind Intensive. Fresh from learning to change my blueprint and programmed beliefs, and now having techniques and ideas to move me financially forward, I finally decided to say it out loud, that my goal is to be a millionaire and why. I thought I heard a snicker.

And then I heard some serious encouragement from some of them. Can you imagine what I was feeling? And then, someone tells me they are sure that I can do it.

Someone here believes in me? And another one does. Whew! What a lesson. I was not confident to say it and then once I did it was like telling myself that I was going to do this thing. It became very real. I had secretly thought I might be judged unworthy! Then came the realization that I had to believe it with all my heart.

This is *my* dream and it only matters what I think. I became my own biggest supporter and cheerleader! I learned who was supportive and safe to be around. Why take advice from other people and have them live your life for you? These people could be stressed out or have personal issues. Most people are so caught up in conforming, they want to live a life of supposed to do's and they want you to do the same. It is a different matter with those you trust, like your Mastermind partners and accountability partners. You already know the people who support you emotionally. You know the safe ones to tell. More importantly, you can make your own choices. Go with your heart.

Feed your dreams. Life always goes on. In the meantime have a good time with it. As to making a list, you may ask why put it in writing? That is because the written word is powerful! It is another way for your brain to process the information.

Let's develop this. First, I'd like you to make a general list. Put your needs and desires down quickly before you have time to analyze them.

Here are some examples:

Bills paid	$500K in the bank
Medical insurance	A new house
Clothes	A new car
Mortgage paid	Trips
Contentment	Barn
Organized	Tractor
Confidence	Art studio

As you can see, this list has a wide range of desires. Taking it to the next level we'll get more clarity on these by being more specific. Now with your list get as specific as possible, for instance which bills? What amounts? What kind of barn? What kind of house and car? A trip to where exactly? Being specific helps you to better visualize what you're dreaming about. The better you can imagine what you want, the faster it manifests! Next, let's turn the list of your desires into positive statements with detail. Your list is gaining more and more clarity and aides your visualization to speed up the process of manifesting.

So, now your list looks something like this:

I live in a comfortable waterfront house.

I have plenty to spare and plenty to share.

My income is $20,000 a month, every month.

I feel healthy and my immune system is strong.

I feel happy and I am at peace.

I am organized.

I love to drive my new Kubota tractor.

I have a barn on my property.

I have my own art studio.

What would you ask for if you knew you could have anything you want?

Okay, let's get even more specific and be descriptive! The more detailed you can be in your description the better you can imagine it, creating a clearer mental image and a clearer vibration, which attracts it to you that much faster...

Here are a couple of examples:

I have a 30-ft x 60-ft barn on my property with a feed room, a tack room, 2 stalls, and an air-conditioned workshop. My tools all have a place and my workspace is organized.

I love my 20- ft x 40-ft art studio next to my house, with high ceilings, heat and air conditioning, north light, shelving, paper drawers, many windows and lots of light. I love to paint and create in here.

You get the idea.

> **The more descriptive it is,
> the better you can picture it.**
>
> **The better you can picture it,
> the easier it is to feel it.**
>
> **The easier it is to feel it,
> the quicker it manifests.**

Every morning, read your list of statements. After reading each one, pause for a moment and imagine already having it. Feel appreciation for having it.

**What would you do if you knew
that you could have anything you want?**

This is not easy for some people because of life's programming and family beliefs. If you could have anything at all, what would you really like to have in your life? Think big! Be honest!

Of course, it is okay to want money! If it is money you want, then ask yourself what you plan to do with the money. This is important. Be specific about the amount and the reasons. Your reasons are your underlying "feelings" about the money. Ask yourself what "feeling" the money gives you. We'll talk more about that later.

WHAT'S UNDER THE MONEY?

Money is good. It helps you to be free to live the life that you've always wanted, to live the life that you've always dreamed about. We have been conditioned to think that it is not okay to desire money; that it makes us selfish. What have you been taught to believe about money? This is the small voice in your head that overrides what you want to believe, but don't. Oftentimes your beliefs about money are ingrained in you from the beliefs of your parents and what they modeled. You were definitely imprinted when you were young by the adults in your life and what they were taught and what they believed. Things like, "It's a sin to have money." Or, "It's not right to spend money on myself." Or, "I must put the happiness of others ahead of my own or people will think badly of me." When the reason for your actions is to avoid being called selfish then you are making a decision that can restrict the possibilities of your own happiness.

It's understandable that you may have the urge to give everything to the people who are important to you and that can lead you to think that giving all of the time is the key to your happiness. Are you doing it to make others happy? Are you assuming it makes others happy? I understand that giving makes you feel good and you may have certain feelings about the act of giving. Have you ever thought that other people want to be good givers too? When you become a good receiver you are giving as well. You are giving others the opportunity to be good givers.

An online dictionary defines selfish as "concern chiefly or only of oneself". To me, that is more self-'centered'. Why would anyone want to encourage such a quality? Well, what if you looked at this differently and defined 'selfish' in a new context, more beneficial and more positively? What if the definition means 'self-secure'? That would change everything. It would be more like knowing what you want and what you expect. When you embrace this meaning it becomes a win-win for everyone.

When you fly you are told in the announcements that if your oxygen mask deploys to put yours on first and then help others. Think about that for a minute. If you give others the oxygen first, then you are "saving" them but not yourself. Why? If you put yours on first, you can help more than one person; because you have the oxygen to draw on to do so. So, I say, be selfish! Feed the "self" first because you need to have something to draw on to give others. It allows you to be more generous and supportive than ever because you can afford to be. And besides that, you absolutely deserve it!

Let's develop your selfishness muscle. Your gifts and talents need nourishment to blossom fully. You can be a good steward of your gifts and talents by creating a setting where they flourish. Then you, along with others, benefit and profit from them. To begin, start by rewarding yourself. It costs less than you think; treat yourself to something simple, an afternoon in the park, an ice cream outing, a matinee, a picnic, a boat ride, a shared experience, etc. Treating yourself is powerful and helps you to feel self-love, which is everybody's right. As you practice being selfish in the best possible sense, you attract more wonderful things because you are in a positive feel-good vibration. Do something good for yourself! Treat yourself as you would treat others. I like to buy flowers for myself. Why wait and hope someone gives them to me? That sets up an expectation. I have more flowers around me because of it and it makes me feel good. Here are some ideas to get you started:

- Identify and eliminate something stressful.

- Create a new daily ritual - a half hour in Nature, or an afternoon tea time (or tee time)

- Time with those who matter like sharing dinner with favorite people.

- Something pleasurable.

- Say, "No" – N O stands for Nurturing Ourselves.

- Something wonderful to look forward to.

This exercise helps you develop positive feelings about yourself, the right kind of selfishness. The more you do these things the more natural they become and the better you feel!

**I choose to live a life filled with joy
and abundance.**

_ _s, it is a choice! Quantum physics demonstrates how our thoughts create our reality. Movies that help you understand this are:

What The Bleep Do We Know?

www.WhatTheBleep.com

The Secret

www.TheSecret.tv

The Shift

www.theShiftMovie.com

The Celestine Prophecy

www.theCelestineProphecyMovie.com

You Can Heal Your Life

www.YouCanHealYourLifeMovie.com

These are just a few of many awesome movies about how our thoughts create our reality. What's reality? Whatever it is to you. This is *your* life and your truth. You have created it with your thoughts. Because your thoughts create your reality, you actually live in a virtual reality. Similar to online assistants, known as virtual assistants, our virtual reality assists us to live our lives in and from the place that our thoughts have created. Stay with me here and I'll explain.

When you look upon something, you see it from your current reality. Remember this – two or more people can look at the same thing and each one has a different "take" on it, a different interpretation based on their own reality – their beliefs and experiences. Have you ever noticed anything like that? When kids play the game "telephone" and pass along a message whispered from one person to the other, usually the last person has a very different description than the one who started it. And that is just hearing it and interpreting what they have heard and then passing on their interpretation of what they heard. When you add in all of the senses, the brain, our internal computer, interprets the information based on the input it has received. From our beliefs and the teachings from our elders, to the variety of information today that is imprinting us from the social networks, our minds interpret this and we pass on our interpretation. We may pass this on through modeling it for others, or discussing it quite often.

Step One Summary

- What are your heart's desires?

- Put everything on your list that you want.

- Feed your dreams.

- The better you can visualize what you want, the faster it manifests!

- The more descriptive it is, the better you can picture it.

- The better you can picture it, the easier it is to feel it.

- The easier it is to feel it, the quicker it manifests.

- What have you been taught to believe about money?

- Your gifts and talents need nourishment to blossom fully.

- Treat yourself as you would treat others.

- This is your life and your truth. You have created it with your thoughts.

"See yourself living in abundance and you will attract it. It always works, it works every time with every person." ~ Bob Proctor

TWO: SEE...

Visualize. Rehearse your future.

Visualizing is using your imagination to see a picture in your mind of what you desire. Visualize what you want in your life. See it as clearly as you can. Look at the details; be clear about it down to the last detail. Be honest and be courageous. Release yourself to grow and be all that you can be.

You may desire ANYTHING. It only takes a little time each day to visualize yourself as already having what it is you want. It is important to visualize every day. It gets you in the flow of positive thinking and positive focus. When I am what I call "in the flow", I feel like anything can happen. I can create some awesome things out of nothing!

> *"You can start with nothing. And out of nothing,*
> *and out of no way, a way will be made."*
> *~ Dr. Michael Bernard Beckwith*

In the past, when I was practicing these techniques, there was a time when I wanted a house. I owned some land and thought the bank would lend me the money to build a house. However, the banker reminded me that I had to have more equity built up, and knowing what I did about creating in my mind first, I decided to manifest that house in spite of appearances.

First, I believed I could have a house. In my thoughts, daydreams and meditations I would create the feeling of what it would feel like to be in my own house. Then I studied my land and decided where the house would be located. This took a little while and as I was doing it I became more connected to my land. I imagined all of the aspects on the land around the house, the driveway and the entrance, etc.

After choosing the ideal location, I put four stakes in the ground to represent the house. To help me feel what it would be like to see the views from inside my house, every day I would stand within that rectangle, look around and say,

"This is the view from my front door."

"This is the view from my back door."

As I gazed upon the view from my house I would listen to the birds singing and smile and be grateful for my house.

Pay attention and be alert to signs, dreams and intuition. One night, I had a dream of a house for sale to be moved. That's a good idea, I thought! I went right to the bank and this time they said 'maybe'. So, I started to look for one. After contacting house-moving companies I saw lots of houses to be moved. One day, while driving through town, I saw a house jacked up and for sale to be moved! It had great potential, so off I went to the bank again. This time they said yes! And, you know what? When that house was moved to my property I had instant equity. And...it in exactly within those four stakes! By the way, I realized that I had arbitrarily placed those four stakes to represent the house. I highly suggest if you do this you may want to choose the exact size you desire the house to be, because you get exactly what you ask for, consciously and unconsciously. Practice seeing your desires come true. Use "tools" that spark you.

Here are some ideas:

- See yourself doing, being and having what you want.

- Daydream. Take some time every day to daydream about already having what you want.

- Notice when others have what you want, what they look like. This helps you to refine your list.

- Listen to motivational and inspirational media.

- Join online and offline groups of like-minded people. (Like PositiveTribe.com and WomensProsperityNetwork.com or a local community group like Meetup)

- Create a Vision Board.

A Vision Board is a board on which you put pictures representing your dreams and positive statements to re-mind you to hold your visions of a happier, healthier, wealthier you. In other words, you are retraining your mind hence 're-mind', another word for mindfulness. The idea is to have a place where you are visually re-minded of your heart's desires and place it where you can see it everyday. For the board you can use corkboard or cardboard or even paper.

There are many places on the Internet to find out how to create a Vision Board. It is very simple and so very powerful.

Basically you:

- Find pictures that represent your desires and stick them onto a board.

- Add words and phrases, too.

- Place this board where you can see it every day.

You are making a statement to the Universe in pictures and words, and it is a visual statement for you. I recommend that you put a picture of yourself in the center of the board. This is all about creating your new reality and you want to be in the picture, right? Place your Vision Board where you see it everyday. Move the placement of your Vision Board every month to shift up the energy and keep it fresh in your mind. You can also refresh the pictures at any time, adding new ones or moving the ones you have around or replacing old ones when you change your mind.

Our brains respond to visual images. The pictures cause us to respond with emotions, which cause us to take action. Use images and words that represent your heart's desires, what you really want. Do the images help you to feel good? Choose your images with care. Remember how my house fit exactly within the stakes that I had put in the ground? Did I limit the size of my house? I believe had those stakes been farther apart then my house would have fit into that larger space.

"Imagination is everything.
It is the preview of life's coming attractions."
~ Albert Einstein

Your imagination is your workshop where your dreams are fashioned. Picture yourself as already having achieved your goals. See yourself doing the things that you'll be doing when you've reached your goals. When you visualize your goals, you get your subconscious mind working toward making your mental pictures come true.

Energize your seed thoughts, your choices, with visualization. In nature, when you plant a seed, you grow a plant and then you harvest the results. When you don't pay attention to seed thoughts, your outcome is vastly different than if you nurture your seed thoughts with actions while believing in the positive outcome that you desire. If you expect a harvest, you nurture the seeds with water and nutrients, and when they became seedlings, you continue to nurture them with water, weeding and feeding. Only then your expectations of a good harvest manifest with extraordinary results. The nature of all energy works the same way.

You may have been trained to pay attention to details and the 'how' of doing things. This is new information and it may take some time to totally 'get it'. You get better at it with practice and that is what these exercises are for. Accept where you are now and know that you are growing into a new You. Rather than worry about HOW something happens, focus on WHAT you want to see happen. This shifts your energy and your results.

From wherever you are right now, you can only see a short distance. When you take a few steps forward you can see farther, and with a few more steps you can see even farther, and so on. That is what happens when you expand your dream and your vision. Each step that you take allows you to see it larger and quicker. If you feel resistance about moving forward, take the time to imagine and see what you want and get your mind back on track. Keep your focus upon your dreams. Dream big, and then watch your creation come alive. Amazing things start to happen when you give as much energy to your dreams as you do to your fears.

"What were you born to be? Not to own, but to be? What do you dream of for yourself and for the world?" ~ Kelley Rosano

Step Two Summary

- Visualizing is using your imagination to see a picture in your mind of what you desire.

- Pay attention and be alert to signs, dreams and intuition.

- Practice seeing your desires come true. Use "tools" that spark you.

- Take some time every day to daydream about already having what you want.

- Listen to motivational and inspirational media.

- A Vision Board is a board on which you put pictures of your dreams and positive statements.

- Your imagination is your workshop where your dreams are fashioned.

- Accept where you are now and know that you are growing into a new You.

- Amazing things start to happen when you give as much energy to your dreams as you do your fears.

"Everyone has inside him a piece of good news. The good news is that you don't yet realize how great you can be! How much you can love! What you can accomplish! And what your potential is!"
~ Anne Frank

THREE: BELIEVE...

Believing is seeing!

If you believe that something is never going to work, then it never works. If you believe in miracles, then you experience miracles. Teach yourself to believe in possibilities and to believe that what you want is already on its way to you. It was easier to do when you were a kid, probably because kids are more open to possibilities. Remember in Chapter One, when we talked about pretend play? As children, that's how we exercised our imaginations.

When I was young, I informed my mother that I knew it was the parents who secretly put out Easter baskets, and that there really was no Easter Bunny. I prattled on about the girl across the street who had provided this information. After a pause, my mother said that she wished I still believed. She told me that she understood that I was growing up. Still, she wished I still believed because only those who believed would get an Easter basket. And, now that I was growing up, she knew that I would understand when the other kids got an Easter basket and I didn't. She smiled at me and turned away. Easter was a big deal in our very large family with eight kids. And the other kids were going to get Easter baskets. I thought a lot about it that night. I weighed the options. I would have to believe if I was going to get an Easter basket. All of the other kids believed, so perhaps it is true. And then I went to sleep that night believing that the Easter Bunny just might exist. I awoke the next morning delighted with the Easter Basket I received.

My mother loved to remind me that the next morning she could hear me running through the house yelling, "I BELIEVE! I BELIEVE!" To this day when fear and doubt creep into my mind, I think of my Mom smiling at me when she said that I had to believe. It really is that simple.

So, wherever you are right now, take a moment and 'see' your dream in your mind's eye. Get to 'know' it and believe!!!! When you believe it, you see it.

"When you believe it, when you can feel it,
it will show up for you. That is the Truth."
~Dr. Michael Bernard Beckwith

This is true for anything you want to manifest. After manifesting my 'dream' house I continued to see and focus on what I wanted to manifest. One of the things that I wanted was a brick patio that I had designed to be a part of the entrance to my house, which was under renovation. All of my funds had to go to the essentials, and bricks were not on the list. Since visualizing worked for the house, I got right on it.

I staked out my patio area and when anyone came by I

would point to the area and say, "This is where my patio made from old bricks is going to be", and I would go on to describe it and show my design. I did not have the old bricks that I wanted to use for this patio, only the idea, so I just affirmed and believed that the patio would be made out of old used bricks.

Be alert always! It creates inspired thought and ideas. I was always alert for old bricks. One day I was driving by the remains of an old house. The chimney was the only thing standing. I thought, "God, I sure would love to have those bricks for my patio." But, I couldn't just take them. So I let go of the idea and drove on. A few days later, I happened to drive by the chimney again and had the same thoughts. Those bricks would be perfect for my patio. Well, I didn't know who owned them so, once again, I let go of the idea and kept on driving. A week later I went by again and desired the bricks. Then I noticed a truck at the empty building next door. Hmmm...maybe there was someone in there who would know who owned the property.

When I have inspired thought, I act on it.

I circled back to the building. As I was walking towards the door, a woman was coming out.

"Hi", I said to her, "is this your place?"

"Yes." She said, "Have you come for the bricks?"

My jaw dropped. I told her that I did, but how did she

know? She said, "I've been praying someone would come and get those bricks because the city is going to clear the lot on Monday."

It was Saturday. I told her I would love to have the bricks and went to get a rope and some help. I pulled that chimney down and now I have a beautiful patio made from old bricks in my entrance. I focused on the end result; a patio made from old bricks, and did not get stuck in the 'how', looking for the money, figuring out how I was going to build it. I could not have planned or imagined how the bricks would show up and that they would come to me so easily and for free.

~~~~~

When we get attached to "how" we would like things to happen, we stop believing and dreaming. Forget the "how"; it happens by itself, you just have to know what you want and stay focused on it. Be a conscious chooser. Keep revising your list of what you desire to do, be, and have. And, know it is happening NOW! You deserve all good. Keep yourself motivated. This is a new habit you are cultivating. You are the only one who can do this for yourself. And you are the only one who can sabotage you. Find creative ways to get around judgmental thinking, yours included. You CAN do this; you just have to DO it.

"Whether you think you can or think you can't, either way you are right." ~ Henry Ford

If you have been doing the exercises I ha៴ far then by now you have done these things:

- ✓ created your list of desires,

- ✓ have listed the ways you think positively,

- ✓ decided how you can look at things differently,

- ✓ practiced building your dream muscle,

- ✓ expanded your list of desires into positive statements,

- ✓ added details and descriptions to that list,

- ✓ created a list of reasons to uncover your underlying feelings about your desires,

- ✓ practiced seeing your dreams and desires coming true,

- ✓ thought of ways to promote self-love,

- ✓ utilized tools for practicing already having what you want,

- ✓ and you have learned how to make a Vision Board.

Are you with me so far? If you haven't done these things yet, that's ok. Now is the perfect time to start these exercises. And look for ways to stay motivated.

Pay attention to how you feel. When you look at your written list of desires, how do you feel? Do you not believe yourself? Does it make you feel less confident? If so, then therein lies a problem. You must believe it if you want to manifest it. You must also "feel" as you would as if you already have it.

What do you really want? Do you believe you can have it? We are conditioned to our situations in life and most people want things to stay the way are because one more thing may change everything. Many of us settle for much less than we can do, be or have. We accept our current lot in life as the way our life will always be...and if that is the case, then it is so! Many of us just follow along the accepted societal rules that have been modeled for us and taught to us. Choices were made for you. What our parents teach us, verbally and non-verbally, has the greatest impact on us. We unconsciously live our lives along the same lines as those before us. Here's a story you may have heard before and not known its origin. This really happened to me.

When I was a newlywed, I was preparing a ham for Easter dinner. As always, I cut off the end of the ham and placed it in the pan. One of my dinner guests's asked why I cut the end off of the ham. "Because that's the way my mother does it," I replied. And that got me to wondering, so I called my mother to ask her. She said that cooking a ham for ten or more people required a big ham and she did not have a pan big enough for that, so she had to cut it to make it fit in the pan that she had. I had unconsciously believed that I had to cut the end of the ham off to cook the ham properly!

While I was writing this I called my sister and asked her why she thought it was. She pointed out that back then things were measured differently. If you bought a whole ham, the standard was much larger then than it is now. She had another good point, that in the 60's pan sizes were typically in fewer selections of sizes. I had been conditioned to cut off the end of the ham and I believed that was the way it was done. Why do you believe what you believe?

Take some time to analyze your beliefs, and you may find that some of them have no foundation! Upon that realization, your beliefs may change!

"Believe and your belief will actually create the fact."
~ William James

Step Three Summary

- Believe that what you want is already on its way to you.

- 'See' your dream in your mind's eye. Get to 'know' it and believe!!!!

- When you believe it, you see it.

- Keep yourself motivated.

- You must believe it if you want to manifest it.

- Many of us settle for much less than we can do, be or have.

- Why do you believe what you believe?

FOUR: FEEL...

Nothing more than feelings.

"Our feelings are a feedback mechanism to us about whether we're on track or not, whether we're on course or off course. See, it's the feeling that really creates the attraction not just the picture or the thought. ~ Jack Canfield

This quote from Jack Canfield says it all. We can change our reality in an instant by changing the way we feel about things. It is at the feeling level that we create our vibrations and that determines our realities. This is plural because all of our realities are different. We all see things differently based upon our life experiences and our beliefs. Different things make us happy. Different experiences made us who we are today. Since we all had different experiences and events in each of our lives and it made us who we are today, then we are all unique and different. We are made of the same stuff except for our life experiences and thoughts. How do you feel about your life, your relationships, your work, and your home?

What is your passion? What brings you joy? What is your contribution to your community? Who are you? Who are you BE-ing? THAT would be your vibration. I use the word "vibration" because, simply put, every cell in our body has a frequency, which your body changes with your thoughts. Your body gives off a "vibe" of how you are feeling. A vibe is a sense or a feeling you get from a person place, or thing. You feel the vibes from others and you exude a vibe and this is what others feel.

Do you want to live a positive life, and everywhere around you, you see and hear negativity? Are you surrounded by people who are less than positive? Do you try to be positive and think that you aren't getting the results that you want? The daily news and the social media create much noise and distraction for you to process. How can you be positive when you have all of this negativity surrounding you, when your head is filled with less than supportive thoughts? Why does bad news grab our attention so easily? It is fear! Even though it is not happening to us, there may be a fear that it could. We "feel" for victims and what we "feel" becomes bigger in our minds. It becomes real for us.

One of my favorite acronyms for fear is, "False Evidence Appearing Real". See, even when events are not happening to us, when we view it and we "feel" it, it becomes real for us. Think of the difference in how you feel when you are happy and peaceful to the feeling of worry and fear. There is a big difference in how these feel in your body. Understand this: both states of mind release hormones and chemicals in the body to accommodate your body to your thoughts.

What about you? How are your thoughts affecting you?

We can and do attract less than positive things to us when that is what we are focusing on. When fear gets in the way it takes us out of the present moment. How we allocate our attention truly matters! If you are feeling anxious or stressed then remind yourself who you really are – a conscious creator!

If your mental chatter is less than positive, turn it around. What else can you focus on? What can you give your attention to that has the best outcome for you and your family, your health and your dreams? Take the lead and make a list of who and what you want to be. Be a conscious creator.

When you change your thoughts and you change how you feel, that is how you change your reality.

Years ago, when I wanted to manifest a new car, I had to decide what kind of car I really wanted. I thought that I wanted something sporty like a Mazda Miata, so I began imagining what that was like. I really liked the idea of it. A friend, and Mastermind partner, rented one and let me try it out. Oh my, it was little. It was cool, though. I felt like a million bucks in that Miata convertible. I began noticing what it was like to have my hands on the wheel. I put some music on. It was fun and it was cute. Then I began noticing that there was not much space to carry anything, and as an artist I was always carrying many things. But, I liked the feeling, so my definition for my desire for a new car changed to a Miata or something better. Very soon, I was driving an RX7. It came to me easily and quickly because I had a feeling attached to my desire. It was red. It was cool! It was roomy. And it was mine!

After that, someone asked me to help her hold a vision of her having a new car.

"Sure," I said, "what kind of car do you want?"

"Oh, any old car will do", she replied.

"Well, you already have that!" I told her.

She needed to get clear on what she wanted; the make and model of it, the color of it, with the features she wanted. Then she could process, visualize and connect to how it would feel to have her new car. Within a few weeks she was driving her new car, too.

Your thoughts create your feelings and your feelings create your reality.

You may not like some things in your life right now, but I hope you now recognize first, that you brought them into your life, and second, that you have the power to change them. You can manifest anything. Yes, anything! You do it all of the time whether or not you realize it. Whatever thoughts you have going on in your mind, your reality is keeping up. Now that you know this, you can be a conscious creator.

Read the list that you made of your desires and dreams

before you go to sleep. You may also do this throughout your day. This changes your mindset and then all of the statements that you have written come true. Please remember that there is no time factor here. It all depends on the trueness of your beliefs and feelings. Remember also, what you think about comes about, so please pay attention to your thoughts.

When you can get to the feeling level of having your desires, then they manifest.

For the most part, I think it is important to keep your goals to yourself so as not to disperse the positive energy. When you tell others, you open yourself up to comments. Tell only those you know who can help you hold the vision.

I invite you to create a Mastermind group or find a partner to help you and each other by holding your vision and their visions, too. A Mastermind group is a small group that you meet with for the purpose of reinforcing growth and success while offering support to one another. Your group's concentration is specifically on personal growth and manifesting success in finances and relationships. In his book Think and Grow Rich, Napoleon Hill defines a Mastermind group as, "coordination of knowledge and effort, in a spirit of harmony, between two or more people for the attainment of a definite purpose."

Mastermind groups visualize personal goals, create intentions and share resources. Being in a group like this helps you to live your life in a state of purpose and aligns you with your talents and your mission. You'll be amazed at what you can accomplish and create. This helps you create a new vibration of yourself and brings satisfaction and significance to your life. Living a life of purpose creates happiness and contentment for you and spreads to those around you. You can accelerate the process by accessing the power of a Mastermind group. The members help you hold your vision, especially when you have difficulty with that. You also feel supported, as the main goal of a Mastermind group is to support one another. It is recommended to have six or less members in your group to keep your talks in a timely fashion. Your meetings or phone calls are to be kept to discussing your goals, missions and purpose and to support one another in that. When someone tells you their goal or dream you can then affirm the goal for them and tell them you see them accomplishing this thing they are wanting. Come to your meetings without judgment and give every person your full attention as they tell you what their dreams are. You can chitchat after your meeting. I hold my Mastermind meeting as sacred space. I am being given an opportunity to support someone in receiving their heart's desires.

How you feel about yourself is very important to your success. How do you feel about yourself? The main reason that some people have an inadequate self-image is because of past conditionings and what they have been taught. They may have feelings that they are not good enough, or worthy of, the things that they desire. If that is true for you then...

This belief has to change.

It is time to condition yourself to believe that what you want can be yours. Seriously, it does not matter about the appearance of not having enough in your life. When you put your focus on your heart's desires, the universe rearranges to accommodate you.

You get what you want by what you are feeling. Be absolutely honest and serious when you analyze how you are really feeling.

WHAT WOULD YOU LIKE TO FEEL LIKE?

Practice! What does it feel like to have what you want?

Do you feel prosperous?

Do you feel grateful?

Do you feel happy?

Do you feel like celebrating?

Do you feel like jumping up and down with joy?

If you want to feel better then PRACTICE! Practice feeling the way that you *want* to feel. If you have a challenge with this then go back in your memory to a time when you felt happy about an experience and relive that experience in your mind. When you recall that feeling by thinking about it you are putting yourself in the vibration of feeling happy and thereby opening yourself up to receiving more happiness. Get to a happy feeling by thinking back to a time in your life when you were joyful, when you felt ecstatic, when everything was going well. Perhaps it was when you bought your new house, or your new car or perhaps when you had your first child. Go back and really connect to the feeling and energy you had at that moment and then remember it as you begin to step into a place of more joy and happiness now.

"Once you understand that the way you feel indicates your level of allowing or resisting, you now hold the key to creating anything you desire."
~ Abraham-Hicks

Change your words. Give your words new meaning. For instance, instead of saying you are frustrated, say you are fascinated. Bob Davies says that when something irritates you say, "Isn't that fascinating?" It takes the emotional charge off of it. You are creating a new reality for yourself. You are changing your focus from negative to positive. This raises your vibration. When anything less than confidence is in your vibration – change it! Shift your focus to the FEELING of what it feels like to have what you want.

Being positive is like sex; you don't have to wait until you are an expert to begin doing it.

One of the things I did to consciously raise my vibration was Laughter Yoga. I felt that laughter would help my body to create endorphins and dopamine naturally and that would make me feel happier. As I said before, chemicals and hormones are released in your body based on your thoughts. Your brain is your command center and is always on alert to keeping your body in alignment.

I joined a Laughter Yoga group that for an hour every week, we laughed with yoga poses and did laughter breathing exercises. Our meditation was lying on the floor in a relaxed comfortable position and we started giggling, then laughing and then outright bellowing laughter.

We had one exercise that I especially loved to do. We acted as if we had won the jackpot! We screamed and jumped up and down and laughed and hugged and danced! What an amazing feeling! Wow, you should do that. It feels wonderful! THAT'S the kind of "feeling" that brings abundance in your life. It brought it to mine. Check out www.LaughterYoga.org to find out more. Watch videos on Youtube.com. Do an Internet search to find the nearest Laughter Yoga group to you.

It is true that laughter is the best medicine. What makes you laugh? How about a funny movie or a comedy show? Some good resources are the Internet radio programs that are available like www.Pandora.com. There are many comedy channels to choose from. You can keep one on all of the time! I recommend that you listen to the PG ones, as they are clean and funny. Choose carefully and keep to the high energy ones. Some other suggestions to create a happy, joyful feeling could be listening to favorite happy music, dancing, going out to dinner, eating delicious food, and taking a walk on the beach or in the park. The goal is to shift your energy and get into that happy feeling place.

This would be a good time to make another list. Make a list of all of the happy, positive, humorous things to do that you can think of and then ask others for ideas. The longer you make the list the more you have to choose from! If you feel overwhelmed by changing your life through conscious choice, just start where you are. Just start doing one thing differently. Have you ever tried to turn the steering wheel on a car when it is not moving? I find that it is easier to turn the wheel when the car is moving. Think about how each of those feels. When you are moving towards something, it's easier to turn the "wheel" of your mind and adjust your direction as you go along.

Just start. Take some action towards your goals.

When you change your thoughts, everything changes!

Your life is richer in many ways when you are happy. In his book, *Success Through a Positive Mental Attitude*, W. Clement Stone tells how he began each day, and demanded that his employees follow suit, by exclaiming:

"I feel happy! I feel healthy! I feel ter-r-r-ific!"
~ W. Clement Stone

BE A WINNER.

When people don't feel good about themselves, physically or emotionally, they tend to feel less like the winner they really want to be. When you want to feel like a winner and you hold thoughts of that, you create a vibration that resonates back to you. All too often, though, you are *feeling* otherwise. It is your responsibility to make yourself feel like the winner.

A very easy way is to meditate on it. Let's do a short exercise on it. During this exercise your concentrated focus on feeling good raises your vibration! It resonates outwards and come back to you with your heart's desires. Simple? Yes, it is. Try it. Leave your expectations behind. Try it now. Pick something that you want in your life then close your eyes and see it in your mind. Get to the feeling level...feel it. Take your time. What does it feel like to already have this?

Now feel it MORE. See yourself as already having it; what does that look like in your life? There. You see yourself with it, in it; now look around from that place of having it. What do you see around you? Do you see your hands on the steering wheel of your new car? Do you see yourself in a lounge chair by the pool of your new home? Describe it. In this case describe the house from your vantage point by the pool. Who is there with you? What are they doing? What do you hear? Create the details!

The more detailed you describe it, the more real it is and the quicker it manifests.

Appreciate the fact that you already have what you want. Feel the appreciation! Recognize what that feels like in your body. Now that you are in the space of being with it and having it, be grateful for it! If you had what you want right now, how thankful would you be? Are you understanding that it is the same feeling when you visualize it as when you have it?

Keep your feelings directed on what helps you to realize your full potential. To attract prosperity, meaningful relationships, and happiness and to live your best life, remember to say,

Thank you!

Thank you!

Thank you!

Step Four Summary

- We can change our reality in an instant by changing the way we feel about things.

- We all see things differently based upon our life experiences and our beliefs.

- Who are you BE-ing? THAT would be your vibration.

- How we allocate our attention truly matters.

- Your thoughts create your feelings and your feelings create your reality.

- Read the list that you made of your desires and dreams before you go to sleep.

- When you can get to the feeling level of having your desires, then they manifest.

- Create a Mastermind group. Mastermind groups visualize personal goals, create intentions and share resources.

- Practice feeling the way that you want to feel.

- Change your words.

- When you change your thoughts, everything changes!

- The more detailed you describe it, the more real it is and the quicker it manifests.

"What do you believe about yourself?" ~ Bob Proctor

FIVE: THANKS...

Have an attitude of gratitude.

Gratitude dissolves negative feelings and purifies thoughts. By their very nature, gratitude and negativity cannot happen at the same time. Just as love and fear cannot occupy the same thought space, in like fashion you cannot think positively and negatively at the same time. If you're not happy with your life at this moment, then now is the perfect time to practice gratitude, because it breeds a positive environment. You can begin now being grateful wherever you are in life. Make it a daily practice to be thankful. It may seem like it is not easy to do when times are tough, and then you try it anyway. You may find that gratitude shifts you and you feel happier, which allows you to hold a positive vibration, thereby shifting your reality. You can make a real difference in your relationships, too, when you can come from a happy and positive vibration.

"I would maintain that thanks are the highest form
of thought; and that gratitude is happiness
doubled by wonder." ~ G.K. Chesterton

Start where you are. Dwell on the good in your life. You already have much to be grateful for. What's most important is that you begin and that you make it a priority in your life. You can be grateful for something even during the toughest of times. If gratitude is difficult for you, then take your focus off of not having enough in your life. Think about what you do have; your loved ones, your health, your work. Pick something to be grateful for - a puppy, the sunshine, a flower, the birds singing.

When you are in a grateful state of mind you are in a positive vibration. Be grateful for what you have right now. No matter how much or how little you have in your life right now, when you practice gratitude and appreciation, your life becomes more abundant.

Be grateful for everything. Gratitude changes everything. When we're in a state of appreciation, everything around us is enhanced positively. It uplifts us, makes us feel happier, and expands our consciousness. Then we attract more positive things. Dwell on the good and watch more good come into your life. It's a phenomenon.

We are the creators of our experiences.

What we create in the world, we must first create in ourselves.

Think about who you are. Who are you BE-ing? Direct your vibration towards the YOU that you want to create in your life and be that person. Recognize certain vibrations in others that you resonate with and this creates your community of like-minded individuals. Have a great appreciation for the people that you attract into your life. They are there because you resonate with them. We are all one. What you find less than positive in another could be looked at in your own life. That person is a reflection of your thoughts (yikes!). You are known for your particular vibration - it is who you are, it is what you are demonstrating and it is what you are attracting.

Funny thing about human nature...we know what's good for us and what makes us happy, and many times we don't remember because our attention is fixed upon on what we don't want! What are you thinking?

What you think about is how you are defining your life and what is in it!

What you think about comes about. If your thoughts have been focused on less than positive feelings then shift them. I have found a useful way to do this that may help you and that is - appreciate what you have now! That's one of the secrets to true happiness. It's also the secret to getting more. As you are feeling appreciation you are coming from a positive vibration, you are resonating a positive vibe out to the world and, by the Law of Attraction, positive things must come back to you.

~~~

One day, as I was sitting on the edge of my pool, I watched the ripple effect happen as my hand stirred the still water. The sun was shining so I saw the shadow of the ripples on the bottom of the pool. To my amazement when the ripples hit the opposite side, they then returned back to me underwater as well as on top! I watched the shadow of the ripples on the bottom of the pool as they went on and on. Everything that the ripple hit sent back another underwater ripple.

This was another "aha" moment for me. I did this over and over because it was such a neat example of how our vibration goes out into the world. When our vibrations contact something, they are then reflected back to us on the surface as well as underneath the surface! What we send out comes back to us, like those positive and negative thoughts. That's a mind blower!

Life is a mirror, whatever you focus on reflects back to you. That's all the more reason for you to focus on the good.

Step Five Summary

- Gratitude dissolves negative feelings and purifies thoughts.

- You cannot think positively and negatively at the same time.

- Make it a daily practice to be thankful.

- Start where you are. Dwell on the good in your life.

- Take your focus off of not having enough in your life.

- When you are in a grateful state of mind you are in a positive vibration.

- What we create in the world, we must first create in ourselves.

- What you think about is how you are defining your life and what is in it.

- Life is a mirror, whatever you focus on reflects back to you.

"Say 'thank you' at every turn. Walk, talk, think, and breathe appreciation and gratitude. When you do this, the circumstances in your life will change to reflect your inner state of gratitude and appreciation."
~ Rhonda Byrne

Chapter Three

"Emancipate yourself from mental slavery, none but ourselves can free our minds." ~Bob Marley

TOOLS

When you surround yourself with the right tools, you are heading in the right direction.

The "tools" to use here are things that help you to visualize and accomplish what you want. They are audio and visual reminders like CDs and DVDs, books, affirmations, etc., as well as conferences, seminars, workshops, and masterminding. Using these kinds of tools helps to keep your desires in the forefront of your mind and your reality. There are many teachers out there if you are open to seeing them. Find the ones that resonate with you. Trust your intuition.

Whenever I get in my vehicle, I put on one of my motivational CDs to listen to as I drive. It helps me to get psyched about changing my life. There is always something positive and motivational in my CD player. Positive thinking and personal development CDs are all that I listen to. I totally surround myself with these tools to keep me on track. To give you an idea, here is a partial list of what I call my "millionaire tools":

Recommended CDs:

- The Secret – Rhonda Byrne

- Secrets of the Millionaire Mind – T. Harv Eker

- Money, and the Law of Attraction – Jerry and Ester Hicks

- Hypnotherapy for the Millionaire Mind – Harv Eker (not while driving)

- Leveraging the Universe and Engaging the Magic – Mike Dooley

- Power of Intention – Wayne Dyer

- The Aladdin Factor – Mark Victor Hanson and Jack Canfield

Recommended reading:

- You Can Heal Your Life – Louise Hay

- Money, and the Law of Attraction - Jerry and Ester Hicks

- Success Through a Positive Mental Attitude – Napoleon Hill & W. Clement Stone

- Think and Grow Rich – Napoleon Hill

- The Science of Getting Rich – Wallace D. Wattles

- You Were Born Rich – Bob Proctor

- The Power of Intention – Wayne Dyer

- Believe and Achieve - W. Clement Stone
- The Vortex - Jerry and Ester Hicks
- The Hidden Messages of Water – Masuro Emoto
- The True Power of Water – Masuro Emoto
- The Celestine Prophecy – James Redfield

Recommended DVDs to rent or buy:

- The Secret
- What the Bleep Do We Know
- The Shift
- The Celestine Prophecy
- The Yes Movie
- Baraka
- You Can Heal Your Life

Some of the teachers that make a difference in my life:

- Jerry and Esther Hicks
- Jack Canfield
- Mark Victor Hanson
- Bob Proctor
- Louise Hay
- T. Harv Eker
- Alan Cohen

- Wayne Dyer

- Masuru Emoto

- Les Brown

- Nancy Matthews

Join groups and take seminars. On my website, www.CandiParker.com, you'll find a resource page with a connection for free tickets to a Millionaire Mind Intensive!

STATEMENTS

Make statements about what you desire. Put your statements in positive terms and write them down. Make them up as they resonate with you. I am always writing down little reminders for myself on sticky notes and posting them where I remember to see them. Here are some that I use...

Money comes to me easily and frequently.

When I have inspired thought I act on it.

I dictate the vibration I am in.

My life is magical.

What's going good for you today?

A positive thought creates a positive reality.

When I feel it, it shows up for me.

Visualize. Rehearse your future.

I'm a money magnet.

And my favorite one is...

I'm so happy and grateful now that...

This one was on my mirrors and doorways and I would fill in the blank many times a day. This is the statement that I believe was the most powerful for me. I'm so happy and grateful now that... I have a beautiful smile. I love my smile! It makes me feel happy. Now you fill in the blank. "I'm so happy and grateful now that..." Smile at yourself in the mirror while you say it. Tell it to yourself as if you were telling your very best friend. There is awesome power in affirmations and statements. I used post-it note signs on mirrors and doorways. Put your signs where you can see them.

Jack Canfield talks about changing a dollar bill into a hundred thousand dollar bill and taping it to his ceiling over his bed to remind him of his vision for $100,000. That inspired me to do the same and, in fact, when I realized that in my heart I really wanted a million dollars, I put a fake million-dollar bill behind the "$100,000" bill because that is what I secretly wanted. Then I became more truthful with myself and I moved the million-dollar bill in front. As I felt more confident I used just the million-dollar bill.

Your words are powerful and power-filled. They communicate your feelings. They communicate to yourself, to others and to the world what you really believe.

What you think about you bring about.

What you talk about, you create in your life.

I'm going to take this to another level right now. I had read several books by Masuru Emoto about how water can communicate. I particularly like his book "The True Power of Water." He proved, with his research, that water molecules do communicate, with each other and with their environment, which includes us, and we are made up of over 70% water! I found it fascinating and I did an exercise that he recommended as one of my "tools." He claims that the words written on a bottle imprint their meaning into the water. He recommends thanking the water. When you thank the water it shifts its vibration and when you drink it the water communicates with the water in your body. His proof is awesome and after seeing proof and hearing testimonies, I decided to try it. I labeled two plain jars of water, one with "money magnet" and the other with "contentment" and I drank from them every day. I replenished the water as needed. And, while drinking this water, I was consciously in the moment and feeling grateful.

These particular words are what I chose because that is what I wanted to create in my life. You may choose other words when you try this exercise based on your own desires. I still do this and I also have words on my showerhead, my bath spigot, my hot water heater, and my well. Love, Gratitude, Health, Wealth, Money Magnet, Contentment, and Thank You. You may chuckle at this. And, if you are, then let me say this to you - I have what I want!

Do you?

Have a grateful heart. Every morning take a few minutes to think about and appreciate the people in your life. Then appreciate what is coming into your life. This experience alone can fill your heart with gratitude. Practice this appreciation with awareness during your day. One of the easiest tools for shifting your attitude and vibration is keeping a gratitude journal. Oprah said that it was one of the greatest things she had done for her life, and she encouraged her audience to make it a daily habit. Writing in your gratitude journal helps you to focus on the good things in your life, even in the difficult times. Use a notebook or a blank journal and start writing!

Get in the flow of gratitude now. Take a few minutes to focus on at least three things you are grateful for and write them in your gratitude journal. Also, write three things you are grateful for that are on their way to you now. You are in the emotional state now as you come into what you want to receive. So, you get in the state by feeling grateful for what you have and then while you are in that state you become grateful for what you want to come into your life. I do this exercise every morning before I get out of bed. It sets the tone for my day.

Who you surround yourself with is who you become. Break away from the "herd" mentality. Ever hear this saying? "When you want to fly with the eagles, don't hang around with the turkeys." Most times we do hang around with the same people we always have because we become comfortable and accepting of our situation in life and it is mirrored in the way we live.

"If you want things to change, you must change things - your attitude, your habits, the people you surround yourself with." ~ Nancy Matthews

We belong to groups where the members are like us, and it makes us comfortable, i.e., religion, education, support groups, etc. Interestingly, I've noticed that people watch and judge each other. People say things like "where were you?" and "what were you doing?" as ways to ferret out information and then proceed to tell you what they think you "should" do as a way to keep you in line with their thinking.

It makes us comfortable to know we are a part of something. It is human nature. People keep each other in the belief system of their choice because that is what they learned from their parents and their parent's experiences. We all have been imprinted by our elders and then by our peers. These are unconscious agreements we have made with the people in our lives because it is non-verbal and were modeled for us. We drink and eat the same things and we observe the same customs as we were taught. Most people stay in their current situations thinking that it will be like that for the rest of their lives. They make the best of it and do not open themselves to thoughts about what could be a better life, an extraordinary life.

Do people call you up and download their negativity on you? For instance, are most of your conversations with them about what's going wrong? Are their thoughts continually focused on negative events? Are they consumed by them? Do they try to get you to agree with them? First, notice it and then shift; look for and talk about positive things or end the conversation and find something positive to shift yourself.

People question when someone in their group goes outside of their normal behavior. They question and are happy to give you their opinions. It's enough to convince you to believe their point of view. This is why it is so important to surround yourself with positive people and environments and why I created the Positive Tribe. When you hold others responsible for what happens in your life, you are diverting your energy. As you start living more positively you may find that there are people in your life that are watching and waiting for you to forget about it and come back to the fold. Just know that they don't have a clue as to who you really are. They are imprisoned by their own limiting beliefs.

You are a powerful, conscious creator. Set yourself free now. CHOOSE to consciously create. When you find yourself in less than positive situations, ask yourself,

"How can I look at this differently?"

What is positive about it? Find all of the positive aspects

you can. Looking at something differently creates a new and different outcome. Interestingly, many people who have not tried something may be quick to tell you it can't be done! They, unlike you, focus on the "can't" and you are now shifting to focus on the "**can**".

Change Attitude Now = Shift!

Keep an open mind, my friend. A friend shared a story that happened to her. She was on the phone with her childhood friend who lives in New York and who was not on the same consciousness path as her. Because of her habits, her friend would go into survival mode a lot. Her friend's daughter was a junior in high school at the time and wanted to go to college in Florida, which was two years and a lot of miles away. All her friend could think about and talk about was, "I can't afford it" and "There is no money for that." She asked her, "Why are you stuck in the belief that your future financial circumstances are the same as your current ones? You have the opportunity to change that." Her friend ended up opening up to that possibility and took her daughter to Florida to look at colleges. And, her friend ended up getting a different job and making more money so it was possible for her daughter to go to school in Florida. Ultimately, her daughter ended up choosing not to do that. Isn't that interesting? Perhaps it wasn't about going to school in Florida and was just an avenue to take that would shift her friend's future.

Once you embrace the messages in this book and believe in them and start taking action from your new belief system, you can change the course of your future! You can always move away from your current scenario!

"The person who says it cannot be done should not interrupt the person doing it."
~ Chinese proverb

Why is it so important to keep your focus on being positive? Why do you have to work at it? Because...

Energy flows where attention goes.

When you focus on negative things, then negative things are what you attract. If your mental chatter is negative, then quickly find something positive to focus on and your negative thoughts go away. Positive and negative thoughts cannot occupy your mind at the same time!

Energy goes where attention flows.

If you put negative thoughts out, then negative results generate back to you.

If you put positive thoughts out, then positive results generate back to you. Life is fluid and expanding. Sometimes you just have move on to something new. By now you have come to realize how important positive self-talk is. It's one thing for others to have less than positive expectations about you, but when you do it to yourself, then...you are actually sabotaging yourself!

One time I did an exercise that required me to look in a mirror twice a day for 30 days and say 100 times, "I am prosperous." It was like there were two people in my head, my ego and me. The exercise went like this...

"I am prosperous." I said as I looked in the mirror.

"No, you're not." I replied to myself.

"What? I am prosperous."

"Yeah, right." I replied.

"What?!!... I am prosperous."

" Really?" I snorted.

"I am prosperous."

"Look at yourself!"

"I am prosperous."

"Is this what a prosperous person looks like?"

"What?... I am prosperous."

"You're kidding, right?"

"I am prosperous."

"Seriously..."

"I am prosperous."

"This is never going to work."

"I am prosperous."

"I am prosperous."

"I am prosperous."

"I am prosperous!"

Before long I was smiling at myself in the mirror (and posing) as I confidently said, "I am prosperous." I enjoy reminding myself (re-training my mind) that I am prosperous in all areas of my life.

Give it a try for 30 days yourself. Seriously.

ACTION

> *"Actions speak louder than words."*
> *~ Abraham Lincoln*

At the end of the word 'attraction' is 'action'. Jack Canfield tells us,

> *"One hour of inner action is equivalent to seven hours of outer action. That is, one hour of intending, visualizing, creating a mindset, meditating, etc. is equal to seven hours of doing."*

Think about the awesomeness of that! Conscious living is all about working with inner action, which is also known as intention. You must work with your intention. And most of us are unaware. Many people want results without expending the effort! Please take inspired action.

People say that they want to make a lot of money, be successful, be financially free, but 90% of them do not or will not do what it takes and they give up and say, "It doesn't work." Not only do people give up, they create excuses, or they blame someone else or something else because it wasn't what they expected. Everyone wants the prize, and those who are successful must do something for it. The work can be easy!

It's the attention and intention that are important.

The difference between extraordinary and ordinary is the word "extra." Do you think Bill Gates or Oprah put in just a few hours a week to achieve success? Keep yourself motivated by consciously doing something positive towards your dreams everyday.

"People often say that motivation doesn't last. Well, neither does bathing – that's why we recommend it daily." ~ Zig Ziglar

AIR OUT YOUR BRAIN

Take yourself for a walk. Sit in nature. If that is not possible, then take five minutes and close your eyes and imagine yourself somewhere in nature; at the shore, the beach, the mountains, the park, etc. See yourself touching the sand, the grass, the rock or the bark of a tree. Hear the whisper of secrets in the leaves of the trees. Touch. Connect.

GIVE

When you need appreciation, give appreciation, it primes the pump for receiving. Practice random acts of kindness everyday, even something as simple a hug or a thank you. Hold a door for someone, return a grocery cart or pay the toll of the person behind you. You can smile at all you see. Compliment your co-workers. Let someone go ahead of you. Call a friend and listen. Send positive thoughts to others throughout the day. Give a package of stuff to charity. Do more than your job and ask for nothing in return.

Touch someone's life today. One small gesture can eventually touch the lives of millions. It all starts with you. Let's do good deeds with extra special focus! Remember the ripple effect I shared earlier? What you do ripples outward and then comes back to you in unseen ways.

FOCUS

You and I are in charge of our inner and outer happiness by the way we view the world and those around us. When you want to raise your level of conscious awareness, then find something really easy to appreciate and lose yourself in deep appreciation of it. Feel how it changes your mental and emotional states. Take time every day to focus on appreciating what you have now and being grateful for what you are creating.

Appreciate yourself. How you feel about yourself affects your life. You improve your self-image and self-worth when you allow yourself to see the best of yourself, as well as the best of others. I'll bet you know what you don't like about yourself. What do you like about yourself? How do you define yourself? Do you describe yourself by an illness or a negative event? Only use the most positive terms when describing yourself; all of the rest shall dissolve in your vibration. Take the time right now to make a list of 5 qualities you love about yourself.

"Your abundance is a response to your vibration."
~ Abraham-Hicks

As you live and attract a more positive life, you become a happier, more creative person.

You are a Beautiful Being of Light shining
with courage! And You are important.

You are creating a new way of thinking. Spend time with like-minded people. Join online groups that support your new belief system, like PositiveTribe.com. Put yourself around people you want to be like for instance, WomensProsperityNetwork.com. Also, you can find local groups in your area at MeetUp.com. Fly with eagles. You have the ability to create your life. Remember, positive and negative thoughts can't occupy your mind at the same time! How can you be more positive?

Practice, practice, practice!

Choose to feel good!

Notice what you are focusing on. Are you re-telling stories that make you feel good or less than good? You can create whatever you want – just focus on the good and more of the same will be repeated in your life. It may not feel easy to be, and stay, in a 'good' mood when events all around you are causing less than positive emotions to rise up and present themselves. We are constantly showered with salacious stories, horrific events, and fear mongering through the media and through word of mouth.

Staying positive in a negative world is easier than you think. First you have to decide that this is what you want to do. Make a choice to practice being positive.

The way I see it, you have two choices in life. See the world as positive or negative. You can keep digging for positive stuff until you find it. In fact, you can find positivity in anything, if that's what you are looking for! What if you used your energy to find something positive all of the time? What if all you did was look for the POSITIVE in everything? How would your life change?

GO ON A NEWS FAST

You can begin to free yourself from negativity immediately. Take a news holiday. It is important to turn off the TV, and stop reading the newspaper. You need daily doses of positivity instead. I hear some of you say that you need to keep up with what is going on in the world! The world goes on with or without you and if there is something that affects you, someone tells you. There is no need to imprint your vibration every day with the negative "news".

Can you do it for 30 days? Try it!

Are you reacting or creating?

CELEBRATE

Celebrate all of your wins, including the smallest ones. Have a small gathering to commemorate and celebrate, even if it is only two people. Or even yourself. A small win for someone who wants to shed excess pounds is passing up the chocolate cake. You could celebrate that with a pedi! If you make a sale, perhaps dinner out! A small win for someone who wants to be a millionaire is opening up to making phone calls to follow-up. Celebrate it! A small win for someone who wants to attract the love of their life is putting yourself out there, like going to the bookstore and engaging someone in conversation. Celebrate your courage in stepping up and out!

Do it for your family and friends, too. Recognize and celebrate their wins. Celebrate an award or an accomplishment. Celebrating lifts everyone's spirits and builds self-worth.

FEED THE SENSES

Your environment is an expression of your vibration. Look at your living space. What do you feel when you walk into your house? What images do you have? What does it smell like? Define your environment to help you harmonize your "vibe" and your home. Use colors that "feel" good to you. Put up pictures of what you want to manifest. Create a mood that makes you feel good when you enter. Your surroundings affect your vibration.

Choose accent pieces, pillows and bedding in colors that make you happy. Use colors that please you on the walls. Relaxing scents are powerful. Soothing music can activate your vibration. I particularly like ocean sounds and waves crashing on the beach. A vase of flowers and your favorite pictures displayed beautifully stimulates you, raises your vibration and puts you in a state of joy.

CLEAR CLUTTER FOR CLARITY

The Chinese word for the energy that is around and in us is "chi", also known as "qi" (pronounced "chee"). Feng Shui (pronounced "fung shway") is the Chinese art of placement and is a method used so that the chi around you flows smoothly. When our chi flows smoothly around and in us, we are calm and at peace. Isn't that something we are always striving for? Learn about and use Feng Shui to help you set a great vibe in your environment.

When you are calm and at peace, you can see things more clearly and make better choices and decisions. When you are clearer of mind, then you are more likely to be clearer in your environment. If your mind is feeling cloudy and cluttered take a look at your physical environment and you may find that it too is cluttered. Make a shift in your physical space and notice the corresponding shift in your energy. It works both ways. You can shift your physical reality by shifting your thoughts, and creating a shift or a change in your physical environment can change your thoughts and feelings.

It always feels good to have a clean and uncluttered environment. The energy flows unhindered and you unconsciously sense this, which allows your energy to flow easily, too. This is important because in Chinese medicine, pain is "stuck" energy. One way that I serve the world is as an Acupuncture Physician. I help clear people's energy and get them pain free. When their energy flows easily, then they feel good. I followed a Feng Shui tip that had me put my written desire in a silver box and place it in a particular corner of my house. I put a million-dollar bill and a completed deposit slip for that million dollars, into my box... thirteen months later I had it. Use your intuition and your instincts.

One day, a visitor came through the gate of the white picket fence that surrounds my front garden. I watched him come through the gate and turn around and go back through it a few times. When I asked why he did that he said he was trying to figure out why it felt so good to walk through the gate. You don't have to know anything about Feng Shui; all you have to do is "feel" what it feels like. I didn't know about chi when I created that entrance. I just did what felt good because I wanted it to feel good when you walked through the gate. It worked!

Recommendations for you...

- Find tools of inspiration to help you like CDs, books, uplifting music, and art.

- Look for the magic in each moment.

- Write at least three things in your journal every day that you are grateful for that you have now and three things you are grateful for that you are attracting to you.

- Practice five random acts of kindness every day.

- Use the power of words – put signs around to remind you.

- Monitor your mental and emotional states often.

- Teach what you are learning by living it.

- Seek out people who can uplift and inspire you

"What people have the capacity to choose,
they have the ability to change."
~ Madeline Albright

You can choose to be positive or negative. It is a choice. Thinking both at the same time is impossible. Every morning remind yourself of your intention to improve your life, and take an inventory every night of how you did that day. Then, in your mind, visualize that your next day is everything you would like it to be and see what happens.

You are powerful because you have the ability to choose in every moment.

Remind yourself every day to be positive, review your day every night, and visualize your next day as being completely positive. Just remember to do it. Perhaps you can put a visual reminder on your bathroom mirror or on the inside of the front door. I had positive reminders on post-it notes all over my house that all led to getting the things that I wanted. My environment is rich with positive words. Keep positivity in the forefront of your mind. The more you practice anything, the better you get.

It's a funny thing about human nature...we know what's good for us, what makes us happy, but many times we forget because our attention is on what we don't want. Stay as positive as you can, raise your vibration, and you attract the flow of prosperity.

Say what you mean and mean what you say.

What if you feel like you're making it up? Of course you're making it up! You always were. Now you are consciously making it up. Think positively! It's a choice. You CHOOSE what you think about and what you talk about. Only you. Remember the power your words have. Have you ever told someone not to do something only to watch them go on and do it? When I began to notice this phenomenon I tested it at the grocery store. I asked the bagger, "Please don't make the bags heavy." They will look right at me and say, "OK." Invariably, the bags were heavy! How is this possible? I practiced it many times and 99% of the time my bags were heavy. So I decided to turn it around and I began to say, "Please make the bags light." Bingo! It worked. It worked all of the time.

All you have to do is form your sentences in a positive manner. Remember, positive words make you feel good. Your words have power so choose the good ones. Only you can choose for yourself.

Look only at positive results. They are the ones that you want to hold in your mind. If you want people to treat you as you want to be treated, what does that look like to you? More importantly, what does that feel like to you? You are free to re-write your script at any time.

*"The people you encounter are actors in the movie
you have written". ~ Alan Cohen*

Make a list of personal qualities you want to manifest
and then turn each one into a positive statement. Here are
some ideas:

I am generous.

I have plenty to share and plenty to spare.

I love to make people laugh.

My happiness is evident and people feel good
around me.

I always choose positive words.

I always look for the good in every situation.

I attract positive situations and positive people into
my life.

I unleash my creative power.

You have to do it yourself. Only you can think for
yourself, no one can do it for you. Be the magnet of a better
life. What do you have to gain? It is far easier to create a
wonder-filled life than you may think.

*"You are in the most powerful moment of your life
right now... as you make the decision to transform
your life forever!" ~ Yvonne Oswald*

Thoughts held in mind produce after their kind.

Don't you always give time to what you believe is important? If you say you do not have time to work at something new, what you're really saying is, "I don't think this is important." Actually, this is the most important work you ever do. When you create a new life for yourself, you are creating a new life for your loved ones, too.

CREATE THE POSTURE

When you feel less than positive you tend to hold yourself in a way that expresses this, there may be a frown on your face, your arms may be crossed and you may be hunched over a little and perhaps you are always looking for what is not good.

When you feel positive the feeling you have is more expansive, and it's reflected in your posture. When you are more positive you hold your head up higher, you stand up straighter, you may have a relaxed face or a smile, you are positive and more open. You have heard the phrase 'keep your chin up' which is a way of saying stay positive! And, when you actually put your chin up it shifts everything. Your body gets more upright and being that way allows your body to function more properly. The blood flows better and the energy flows better, which means better health and a better feeling about your health.

While you are reading this, check yourself out. How are you sitting? Pull your shoulders back and notice the difference. It's a different feeling in your spine and the chest when you pull your shoulders back.

Sit up tall. When you sit up as tall as you can, you open up your spine. This allows your spinal fluid to flow better bringing the nutrients it carries to your whole spine that sends messages to your whole body. It allows a better brain/body connection, and better circulation creating a clearer mind, a happier heart and a peace-filled body.

A simple thing like sitting tall or standing tall allows your system to flow better, run better, and serve you better... allowing you to be fully present in your life. Be conscious of it. Feel it open up your energy.

SHOULDERS BACK!

SIT UP TALL!

Now, in this position, sense what your face feels like. Are you smiling? Smile right now and feel how that changes your face and your vibration. The act of smiling creates messages in your brain to release the happy hormones, so you actually feel better when you are smiling. And when you're smiling, the whole world smiles with you. (Are you singing?)

Make a sign with these words and post it where you can see it in your environment to remind yourself.

SHOULDERS BACK!

SMILE!

Can you feel the difference? Here's a way to practice... Before you answer your phone, consciously put a smile on your face and the vibe you emit when you say "Hello" has a smile in it. I call it paving the way. Place a "SMILE" sign next to the phone. When you smile into the phone the caller can sense it, and it keeps the tone of the call positive.

Every day is an opportunity to grow and do better. Believe it. Believe in yourself. Develop the posture of success and happiness, and you create a new reality for yourself and your loved ones. I want you to create this for yourself.

SMILE MORE!

I know as you've been reading this some of the ideas and suggestions are easy to accept and some not as easy. What are you willing to accept so that you can grow? All you have to accept is that THERE IS ANOTHER WAY of looking at and living life. Ultimately your choices are what separate you from everyone else. Choose what you want. Expect and accept the best. Dream big!

Dreams are wonderful things. They can propel us to happiness and add passion and give our lives meaning and purpose. Perhaps people have forgotten their dreams because they think they won't be successful. They may have tried before and was unsuccessful and they carry that memory with them. Or, perhaps they have believed those people who told them their dreams are unrealistic or even silly. We all have our reasons, excuses, fears, and doubts.

eserved for nothing.

But when these things keep us from reaching our highest potential, it's time to step up and take control. What have you missed out on, or are now missing out on, because fear or doubt stopped you? Move forward. Change your reality and situation today.

> *"Every great dream begins with a dreamer.*
> *Always remember, you have within you the strength,*
> *the patience, and the passion to reach for the stars*
> *and to change the world. " ~ Harriet Tubman*

Teachers are attracted into your life to help you create the life you want. You've already begun doing this by reading this book. Stay in the flow, stay in the conversation and more teachers appear and you, too, shall become the teacher for others. Make new friends. Surround yourself with people who believe anything is possible. Take action. Believe that you DO know what you're doing. YOU are the creator of your own destiny. Choose to be happy each and every day. Be open to learn something new. You create what you want to create... so create your own success. Do you have a great idea? Give it life! When I have an inspired thought I take action. Remember the story of the bricks for my patio? When you make being positive a priority in your life, you appreciate life more. When you appreciate life more, you create more abundance and happiness. When you are grateful every day...

Shift happens!

Whatever has happened to you up until now know this, NOW is NEW. Be aware and shift when you need to.

When you improve yourself, you improve the world.

Practice, practice, practice. If you were going to give a concert, you would practice. If you were going to play in a tournament, you would practice. If you want a better life, then practice!!! The more you practice, the better you get. You can have whatever you desire if you see it, feel it, and believe it.

Choose. See. Believe. Feel. Thanks.

Circumstances challenged me, but they did not stop me. I imagined a better situation and a better life for myself, and used the power of my positive imagination to make it happen! From poverty-stricken widow to happy millionaire through the power of positive thinking, I now live a life people may only dream about. Suppose you could have what you want. How would that change your life? You could work from home, get to travel when and where you want, have financial success, live the way you want to, and get to focus on what matters most to you. What kind of life will you have? Imagine that this is the time that you break through your own barriers. This is where you decide whether you'll embrace the life you were meant to have.

Epiphany – an intuitive grasp of reality through something - usually an event or an illuminating discovery, a revealing scene or moment, a change.

You are the only one who can create a new life for yourself and give your life new meaning and purpose. Step up and be responsible for it. You can create the life you really want.

I believe! Do you?

Here's to your massive success! I want you to truly live the life that you dream of! I encourage you to begin... Right now!

Define. Refine. Align. It's MINE!

Your beliefs shape your future. Listen, it does not matter

where you are in life or what has happened to you. Today is new! There is no time factor on creating your new reality. Start now. You may not realize it yet, but the fact that you have read this far tells me that you want to change your life. In spite of ALL appearances, your life can change for the better.

"One joy shatters a hundred griefs."
~ Chinese proverb

When new life opportunities present themselves, you can either go with the flow or let them go them. When you resist starting over or starting something new, pay attention to what you are feeling. You may feel all sorts of less than positive feelings and this is your inner guidance system, giving you a nudge to take another look at the situation. Old beliefs and fears, (false evidence appearing real), may be holding you back. Your new life begins in your mind and thoughts.

Ask yourself,

"How can I look at everything differently?"

Starting over is a real opportunity, especially when you look at it as such. Create a new life from where you are right now. Acknowledge and accept that your current reality has been created by your thoughts, most of them unconscious and without specific focus and intention to what you really wanted. Since you are the creator, you can now choose to consciously create a new reality; one based upon what you really want! Keep putting one foot in front of the other, think positive thoughts as often as you can, and visualize what you want your life to look like. Remember...when you hold thoughts of not having enough, you get more of it. When you hold thoughts of having the life you want, it slowly starts to manifest and the more attention you give it the more the things you want appear in your life. Keep it up!

Surround yourself with positive people (even if at first it is only on the Internet). Keep your thoughts, words, and actions focused on your eventual outcome, and it rolls out and unfolds right before your eyes. It is real. You are creating a new "vibration" of yourself through which your desires are "attracted" to you, just like a magnet. It takes time for the people closest to you to accept the new you. Remember, you have to accept the new you first. As you are making changes within yourself people around you start to change and respond and react differently to you. They start vibrating with you - or not.

As you are starting off on your new path, in order to keep your energy and your vibration in a positive state, notice that other people's responses and reactions are influenced by their limiting beliefs and their fears. You can let it go. Be mindful and hold steadfast to your new belief system instead of what people around you may be saying. And seek out people who do believe in you and the universal Law of Attraction.

Commit to making the shift within yourself.

Chapter Three Summary

- Make detailed statements about what you desire.

- Your words are powerful and power-filled.

- What you talk about, you create in your life.

- Looking at something differently creates a new and different outcome.

- Energy flows where attention goes.

- Positive and negative thoughts cannot occupy your mind at the same time!

- At the end of the word 'attraction' is 'action'.

- Attention and intention are important.

- Appreciate yourself. How you feel about yourself affects your life.

- Spend time with like-minded people.

- Look for the POSITIVE in everything.

- Take a news holiday.

- Celebrate all of your wins, including small ones.

- Find tools of inspiration to help you like CDs, books, uplifting music, and art.

- Write at least three things in your journal every day that you are grateful for that you have now and three things you are grateful for that you are attracting to you.

- Practice five random acts of kindness every day.

- Teach what you are learning by living it.

- Seek out people who can uplift and inspire you.

- You have the ability to choose in every moment.

- Say what you mean and mean what you say.

- Thoughts held in mind produce after their kind.

- Be aware of your posture. Smile more.

- You attract teachers into your life to help you create the life you want.

- When you improve yourself, you improve the world.

- You can consciously create a new reality; one based upon what you really want.

- You are creating a new "vibration" of yourself through which your desires are "attracted" to you, just like a magnet.

"How wonderful it is that nobody need wait a single moment before starting to improve the world."

– Anne Frank

Chapter Four

A MILLION BUCKS

If you have been doing what I suggested so far you should be manifesting new things into your life. Let me tell you the story of how I got my money. I attracted it to me. I practiced feeling like a millionaire because that is what I wanted to manifest. I paid attention to everything millionaire. (Yes, even watching "Who Wants to Be a Millionaire.") Every week in laughter yoga I did an exercise where we acted like we won the jackpot and it may very well be the reason that I won a lottery. Who knows? I do know this... consciously applying the Law of Attraction transformed my world.

We all have history that we have decided is less than good and I did, too. When my husband had a stroke I took off from my work for a year to take care of him. When he died all of his income died with him and I found myself a widow with no income. On the day of my husband's funeral one of my brothers was murdered in another country. I was still with my family when we found out. And, while it was very shocking, even at that moment I chose to look at the positive and be an anchor for my family. My brother was the first of the eight siblings to die. I chose to celebrate our brother's life and look for all the happiest memories and share them. In the midst of sadness I remembered this – it's all in how you look at it! I choose to focus on the positive things in my life. As life moved on, I was like many people, just making ends meet, and during that time I chose to be in a happy and positive vibration for my health and mental well being. I would consciously choose good thoughts. With the realization of just how short life can be I decided that my time here must be quality time for myself, my animal companions and for the people around me. Most importantly, I was grateful every day for my dreams already being so. I worked at reducing my debt, living frugally and strategically. Even then, I held positive thoughts and visions of being a millionaire.

It was now three years after my husband and brother had passed away and I was driving home, returning from spending Christmas at a brother's house. I was looking for the least expensive gas I could find and kept searching as I was driving. I finally ended up at a tiny gas station. Being alert has its rewards. While at this gas station, I saw a big poster – 'Holiday Millionaire Raffle. Would you like to be a millionaire?' Why, yes, I would! Anything that had the word 'millionaire' in it got my attention. One of my affirmations was and still is,

When I have inspired thought, I act on it.

The moment came when I had the inspired thought to buy a ticket. I did not ask for, or pray to win the lottery, although you may. And, until then, I never bought lottery tickets!

At this moment, as I mentally asked myself, "Should I buy a ticket?" my puppy started barking very excitedly and was jumping around in the vehicle. I thought he just had to get out, so I quickly took him for a little walk. I thought it strange that he didn't even pee, and then I let the thought go and went back to the car. When he was put back in the vehicle, I thought to myself, "Gee, before I leave I wonder if I should I get one of those tickets?" And, just as I had this thought, my puppy started his barking again – and he was looking throuogh the window intensely right at me! Hmm. Is that a sign? I reached into my pocket and felt the two twenties in there. This was a twenty-dollar ticket! I had a moment as I mentally tallied the balance in my checking account, as my history and old beliefs flooded me with lack thoughts. And then, in the blink of an eye, I shifted. After all, the sign on my dashboard was "When I have inspired thought, I act on it." And, since my puppy had never done this before, I smiled and said, "There's my sign!"

It was three days before the drawing and when I asked the attendant if there were any tickets left he said, "Sure, how many do you want?" Again, I felt the two twenties and then, with a smile, I said to him, "Just one, and make it a winning one!" I could not choose the number I got because it was a statewide raffle and you got the next available number. OK, I told myself, this was a Christmas present to me and I kissed the ticket, gave thanks to it for winning and then tucked the ticket in my visor and forgot about it.

I paid attention to the signs. I checked in with my intuition and when fear showed up I released the fear and I moved forward in faith and the belief that this was a good thing for me because I could feel a good feeling inside of me. My feelings are my guidance system and your feelings can be your guidance system when you pay attention to them.

A week after the drawing had taken place I finally remembered to look. There were 12 draws for a million dollars each as well as other money prizes. I started at the beginning looking at the winning numbers. On the twelfth and final draw for a million dollars I was startled. Those numbers look familiar. Could it be? I hadn't looked at the ticket since I got it and it was still in the visor of my car. At the time, I was on the phone with a friend and she sensed something, and asked me what was wrong. Nothing! I told her I was just going to walk out to my car to check something. I printed out the numbers. I had to check a lottery ticket. I hustled on out to the car and pulled the ticket out of my visor. I gasped! "What's wrong?" I was asked again. Wait a minute, wait a minute... it looks like I won the lottery! "What?!!!!!" Wait, wait. I painstakingly went over each and every single number to match it with what I had printed out. My mind did not believe it. My feelings were off the chart excited. I told my friend that I thought I had just won a million dollars. She screamed! I screamed! And it clicked! I shouted,

"I JUST WON A MILLION DOLLARS!!!!!"

Can you imagine how I felt? What would you do? After fifteen minutes of yelling "Oh my God" and jumping up and down in the yard I thought, now what? I panicked! What if I'm not right? What if I am right! How do I get this money? It was 3:30 on a Friday afternoon and the Lottery office closed in a half hour and was 25 miles away. I have to protect this ticket now until Monday? My mind was sparking! I put the ticket in a baggie and, very carefully,

rushed to the bank and opened a safe deposit box. Now, can you imagine how I felt all weekend? I wanted to tell everyone! And then I didn't want to tell anyone because what if I am wrong? It was a rush.

When Monday came I had a friend drive me to the state offices of the Lottery while I held on to the ticket in the baggie with two hands as if it were the most precious thing in the world. This friend owned a flower shop and her car was painted all over with flowers. How appropriate! I had my own single car parade to the Lottery headquarters. So, with two of my friends, I paraded into the lottery office and I was SO relieved to have them confirm the ticket. They handed me a BIG check and we took a picture and headed off to celebrate with another friend at a French restaurant. We had a big time.

My million dollars was delivered through a raffle. The real story here is actually how it was created. It could have just as easily been delivered to me through an Internet Marketing campaign, writing a best selling book, inventing a game, a gadget or a gift.

This book is not about winning a lottery raffle; it's about being in the vibration of being a millionaire to become a millionaire. It is being in the vibration of having what you want!

> You can be in dire straits, and today you can begin to change your life - right now. You have to THINK about it a lot. You have to ACT as if you already have it and PRACTICE feeling grateful for having it. Put your FOCUS on what you want! Keep your ATTENTION on creating happiness.

Maintain your positive thoughts and hold your vision with a grateful heart that it is already so. Be courageous and ready to be all that you are capable of being. Know in your heart that abundance and prosperity are indeed yours!

I believe in you! Your time starts now! Do the exercises in the Workbook in Part 2 of this book. Make your life a happy, positively prosperous one.

If you have a story of a positive shift in your life, I want you to share it! When you share your story it increases the energy you give it in your own life and it increases the energy in the total consciousness. Tell me about it. I want to hear from you about your positive shifts! Drop me an email at: Candi@CandiParker.com.

**Our thoughts, feelings, words and actions are
all forms of energy. What we think, feel, say,
and do in each moment comes back to us
to create our realities.**

You have already chosen to be successful – or you wouldn't be reading this book. If you are doing the exercises, then you have taken a step that most people won't. And you will enjoy the success that many others won't.

Let me be clear.

The Law of Attraction does not come knocking at your door with a truck full of money. You must take some action to shift and change your life. And if you have tried and been unsuccessful before, then you owe it to yourself to try this way.

This book holds the knowledge and the steps that cut

you loose from the constraints that are holding you back from having the life that you really want. You deserve it! I've opened the door for you. It's up to you to take the steps to go through it and you will not be alone.

Take the first step and join the free online community at PositiveTribe.com and declare that today is your day to re-claim and re-create your life.

I invite you to start the Workbook exercises and watch as your life shifts!

Chapter Four Summary

- Consciously applying the Law of Attraction transforms your world.

- Being alert has its rewards.

- When I have inspired thought, I act on it.

- Pay attention to the signs.

- This book is about being in the vibration of being a millionaire to become a millionaire.

- You can be in dire straits, and today you can begin to change your life - right now.

- Maintain your positive thoughts and hold your vision with a grateful heart that it is already so.

- Our thoughts, feelings, words and actions are all forms of energy.

- What we think, feel, say, and do in each moment comes back to us to create our realities.

"So throw off the bowlines. Sail away from the safe harbor. Catch the trade winds in your sails. Explore. Dream. Discover."

~ Mark Twain

SHIFT
HAPPENS

PART 2

THE WORKBOOK

**A Workbook for Living the
Law of Attraction**

Blending Action and Attraction.

Download additional worksheets and more at this page just
for readers - http://CandiParker.com/worksheets.html

By getting to this point you have taken a big step
forward towards creating the life you really want.
Congratulations! Enjoy each step of the journey. You have
made a major decision and it is a big deal. In this section
there is a variety of exercises to help you be and stay on
your new path. Do them.

We create our stories from our beliefs. It is now time to consciously create new beliefs. Here is where you create a new story for yourself on the storyboard of your mind. Your state of mind must be BELIEF and not just wish or hope. You'll only be ready to receive when you BELIEVE you can have it.

Every time you want something, your request shoots to your inner being to become a part of your vibration, which in turn attracts the same, whether consciously or unconsciously. Now it's time to consciously and purposefully create a new vibration, a new reality, for you.

Look around at what you are attracting now. The Law of Attraction is always responding to your vibration. ALWAYS. If you don't like what you see, now is the time to change it. How? You are always drawing to you all things necessary for the manifestation of your requests. Make a decision and your life changes. It happens with intention and attention.

Act like a Hollywood actor as if you are assuming a role. Most people are extras in their own movie. Be the star! YOU are the most important one here. YOU are the only one who can change your life; no one else can do it for you. Are you letting others manage your life? All of your relationships in your life, including your pets, are profoundly affected by your relationship with your Self.

The purpose of this workbook is to help you to get in, and stay in, a positive vibration. These exercises activate all of your subconscious processes, which in turn activate your motivation to make your dreams come true.

You must understand who you are. You are a creator. You can create anything. Your greatest power is your ability to choose. Just having a thought is creating a reality. Everyone has dreams but not everyone takes purposeful action.

"Never change things by fighting the existing reality.
To change something, build a new model that makes
the existing obsolete." ~ Buckminster Fuller

"Stay aligned with your intentions, and your good will find you." ~ Alan Cohen

Chapter Five

"Ideas are like rabbits. You get a couple and learn how to handle them, and pretty soon you have a dozen."
~ John Steinbeck

THE LIST

Let's work on your lists: What do you really want?

Think about what you really want and write it here ...

_____

_____

_____

_____

_____

_____

_____

_____

_____

_____

_____

_____

_____

Your vision is the big picture of your future reality. What is your big picture – how do you want to see yourself in the world?

Example:

> I teach people how they can be and stay positive in a negative world.

My Vision:

_____

_____

_____

_____

_____

_____

_____

_____

_____

_____

_____

_____

_____

_____

_____

_____

What results do you expect?

Examples:

> I joyously play in my 30' x 40' art studio that has north light, lots of windows, paper drawers, high ceilings, great storage space, and a tub sink with hot and cold water.

> I create a foundation to help people become more positive and focus on re-creating who they want to be, do and have.

My Outcomes:

_____

_____

_____

_____

_____

_____

_____

_____

_____

_____

_____

_____

_____

_____

_____

_____

_____

_____

_____

_____

_____

_____

_____

_____

_____

_____

_____

_____

_____

_____

_____

_____

_____

Why are you doing this? What brings fullness and satisfaction and significance to you?

Example: I make a positive difference in millions of lives.

My Purpose:

_____

_____

_____

_____

_____

_____

_____

_____

_____

_____

_____

_____

_____

_____

When you decide what you want it then begins to move into physical form.

Chapter Five Summary

- Make your lists.

- What do you really want?

- What is your big picture – how do you want to see yourself in the world?

- What is your vision, your outcome, and your purpose?

- What results do you expect?

- Why are you doing this?

- When you decide what you want it then begins to move into physical form.

NOTES

CHAPTER SIX

TIME TO CHOOSE

What do you really want to have in your life?

Write it here: (yes, again. Shift is happening.)

_____

_____

_____

_____

_____

_____

_____

_____

_____

_____

_____

_____

_____

_____

_____

_____

_____

_____

_____

_____

_____

_____

_____

_____

_____

_____

_____

_____

_____

_____

_____

You may not have what you want tomorrow – you will have to do a little work. The work you have to do is visualize and feel it.

1. Visualize every day, many times a day.

2. FEEL it.

You have to have a great picture in your mind to really motivate yourself. What do you picture?

Chapter Six Summary

- It's time to CHOOSE

- What do you really want to have in your life?

- Visualize every day, many times a day.

- You have to have a great picture in your mind to really motivate yourself.

NOTES

CHAPTER SEVEN

IMAGINE.

Visualize. Rehearse Your Future.

Let's enrich the picture you are painting of your new reality. In seeing yourself having, being and doing what you want:

- Where are you?

- Who is with you?

- What are you wearing?

- What do you hear?

- What do you smell?

Use all of your senses: touch, taste, smell, see, hear, feel...

Example: I am sitting on a tropical beach in lounges with my sister and my niece. We are having exotic cocktails and sighing and relaxing as we watch the glorious sunset happening as if is just for us. The sky is painted with a golden hue and studded with pink, bronze and lavender clouds in the most beautiful formations. The air is warm with a gentle breeze caressing our skin. I am bonded with my sister and my niece and we smile at each other satisfied that we deserve this.

Describe your desires in detail.

_____

_____

_____

_____

_____

_____

_____

_____

_____

_____

_____

_____

_____

_____

_____

_____

_____

_____

_____

_____

Keep describing your desires...

_____

_____

_____

_____

_____

_____

_____

_____

_____

_____

_____

_____

_____

_____

_____

_____

_____

_____

_____

_____

_____

_____

This is You now consciously creating a new future. Let's take it another step.

When you already have what you want, what do you want your life be like? Describe your ideal life.

Where will you be?

_____

_____

_____

_____

_____

_____

_____

_____

_____

_____

Who is there with you?

_____

_____

_____

_____

_____

Where do you go?

_____

_____

_____

_____

_____

_____

_____

_____

_____

_____

Who is traveling with you?

_____

_____

_____

_____

_____

_____

Where do you live?

_____

_____

_____

_____

_____

_____

_____

_____

What does your new personal space look like?

_____

_____

_____

_____

_____

_____

_____

_____

_____

_____

What do you do during the day?

_____

_____

_____

_____

_____

_____

_____

_____

_____

_____

_____

_____

_____

What kind of people are your friends?

_____

_____

_____

_____

_____

_____

_____

_____

_____

_____

_____

_____

_____

How do you serve the world?

_____

_____

_____

_____

_____

_____

_____

_____

_____

_____

_____

What do you do for fun?

_____

_____

_____

_____

_____

_____

_____

_____

_____

_____

_____

What new habits do you have?

_____

_____

_____

_____

_____

_____

_____

_____

_____

What do you look like? Describe yourself.

_____

_____

_____

_____

_____

_____

_____

_____

_____

_____

What kind of vehicle do you drive?

_____

_____

_____

_____

_____

What color is it?

_____

_____

_____

What does it smell like?

_____

_____

_____

_____

Who rides in it with you?

_____

_____

_____

_____

_____

_____

Do you believe you can have it all? A belief is a thought you think over and over. It's just a thought. Your old beliefs can hold you back from success. Entertain the idea of changing them.

**It is done unto you as you believe,
simply because you believe.**

NOTES

Chapter Seven Summary

- Enrich the picture you are painting of your new reality

- Describe your desires in detail.

- Describe your ideal life.

- A belief is a thought you think over and over.

- It is done unto you as you believe, simply because you believe.

*"If you insist on clinging to who you are right now, you
will miss the next greatest version of yourself."*
~ Debbie Ford

CHAPTER EIGHT

FEEL

"See, it's the feeling that really creates the attraction not just the picture or the thought." ~ Jack Canfield

Your feelings are the key. How you feel is how your reality is created quickly. Your mind creates the picture and your feelings about it give it life. The longer you can hold a positive thought and feeling around something, the quicker it manifests. Jerry and Esther Hicks say that deliberate creation can happen very quickly in 68-second bites. That's 4 sets of 17 seconds. They say if you can hold a thought for 17 seconds it is well on it's way to manifestation.

It's time to try it. Get a visual in your mind and hold that thought for 17 seconds. Not so easy, huh? It becomes much easier when you attach a positive feeling to it. Feel as you would as if you already have what it is you want. When you are imagining something in your mind, see it as if it is right there next to you – as if you can reach out and touch it. Now you are creating on purpose. Now you are being a "deliberate creator".

Chapter Eight Summary

- How you feel is how your reality is created quickly.

- Your mind creates the picture and your feelings about it give it life.

- Hold a thought for 17 seconds it is well on its way to manifestation.

- When you are imagining something in your mind, see it as if it is right there next to you – as if you can reach out and touch it.

CHAPTER NINE

WHAT'S UNDER THE MONEY?

Let's get some more clarity.

When asked what they want, most people say money. Money is good. Money can buy things. Let's look at your reasons and what's under the money.

- Why do you want what you want?

- How do you feel when you have it?

Fill in the blanks with things and experiences money can give you that you would like to have...

I want: Because:

Example: white Cadillac Escalade	It is classy. It makes me feel rich.

I want: Because:

Writing it gives it power. Visualizing on it gives it form. It really helps to define what you want. Do you have a picture in your mind that shows you what it looks like to already have your heart's desire? I want you to take a minute to decide what that picture is for you. Take a few moments, close your eyes and run through pictures in your mind's eye. What picture would you put on the cover of your storybook? Daydreaming is creating. Take a time out right now to daydream.

~~~~~

A word about the 'ripple effect'... When others see you improving yourself, you are not them same as you were to them. They may feel less than supportive and may not want keep up with you. Subconsciously they might do and say things to hold you back from success as a way to keep you at the same level you were at with them. That is so they can relate to you. Or you may find yourselves just drifting apart because you can no longer relate to each other.

What outside things are influencing your motivation? All too often we accept less than positive situations in our lives. Sometimes we feel powerless to control our own lives. What is diverting your energy? Stop allowing yourself to be pulled in many directions, set boundaries, believe in yourself and focus on the direction you would love to have. Whatever you are giving attention to is what you are manifesting. Awareness is power. Changing your thoughts can turn undesirable situations into positive ones.

Someone's opinion of you does not have to become your reality. How we live our lives is the result of the story we believe about ourselves. Prepare yourself emotionally everyday. How are you setting the stage for your day?

At each new level of awareness your conditions, circumstances, and environments change. As you adapt to the changes, you are then able to see the next step and move to a new level of awareness. Yes, you are always learning. It's like driving a car. When you first get in the car you can only see so far and when you drive further on down the road you can see more. It is important to continue nurturing your mind positively and then things start to change. This change happens quicker when you let go of the less than positive thinking. Are you wondering how to think positive when you're not? If your focus is on what is not coming to you, then stop and consciously put your focus on what you want to see. It's a plan.

You wouldn't get in a car and drive aimlessly. You would have a destination. You would know where you are going. You would have a plan. You might not be able to actually see the destination physically as you get in the car, but you know what it looks like, you have expectations of what it is going to look like when you get there and the same thing happens as you drive towards your dreams.

Whatever you're thinking about is literally like planning a future event.

"When you're worrying, you are planning.
When you're appreciating you are planning. What
are you planning?" ~ Diego Reyes

Psychologists tell us that 70% or more of our thoughts are negative and that they take away our power and limit our abilities. Everyday we're showered with negative thoughts and messages and as we continue to absorb them we can create negative thinking patterns. That leads to limiting beliefs! We all have less than positive thoughts! The occasional negative thought has little or no impact. It is the chronic negative thinking that destroys your life.

You may have been supporting and living old teachings that may not be in any way supporting who you really are and who you really want to be. You downloaded information from other people as a kid and now you continue living by it. These are the thought patterns that need to be replaced as soon as possible. You may also be living your financial life based on other people's stories. We learned from our parents and grandparents about how they experienced money. My father and mother always tried to get a discount. They had eight kids! I don't have any kids so why do I always try to get a discount? Because it is learned behavior.

We all have core issues around money.

- How do people in your life talk about money?

- What do they say to each other?

- What do they do when there is tension?

We pick that up. How have your beliefs about money affected your life?

Sometimes you may say things negatively:

- "I make do with what I have."

- "I've got to get a discount."

- "The chase is on."

And positively:

- "I have plenty to spare and plenty to share".

- "My bills are paid in full".

- "Money comes to me easily and frequently".

You think it all into being and your self-talk is an expression of what you are thinking.

Chapter Nine Summary

- What's under the money?

- Why do you want what you want?

- How do you feel when you have it?

- Writing it gives it power. Visualizing on it gives it form.

- Whatever you are giving attention to is what you are manifesting.

- Awareness is power. Changing your thoughts can turn undesirable situations into positive ones.

- Set the stage for your day.

- Consciously put your focus on what you want to see.

- Whatever you're thinking about is literally like planning a future event.

- You may have been supporting and living old programming that may not be in any way supporting who you really are and who you really want to be.

- How have your beliefs about money affected your life?

- You think it all into being.

hift Happens_

NOTES

CHAPTER TEN

BELIEVE

What do you believe about your life? This is important. A belief sets up a vibration through your thoughts, attitudes and emotions that are matched by the Law of Attraction and it is reflected in the people you meet and the situations you are in. You will attract new people and events as you "vibrate" to the new you. Examine your beliefs and see if there are any you would like to change. What new beliefs would you like to create?

My OLD belief	My NEW belief
Example: I can't write a book.	If I just begin I can write a book.

My OLD belief	My NEW belief

Your mind is your most incredible tool. It takes anything you give it and attract its like vibration to you!

When you see something on the screen of your mind that no one else can see, it automatically starts moving into form through your subconscious mind. This is the point where most people cancel their desires. For instance, if you want something and you get a picture of it in your mind, and you daydream about having it – many times the next thought is something like, 'but, I can't afford it', or 'that can never happen to me', etc. In that case, you would have then just totally cancelled having what you desire. And so it is.

When you build an idea in your mind, it sets up an attractive force and you then attract to you the things you need for the manifestation of your idea. That is only if you keep building it in your mind, give it attention and intention, and believe it can be. Some may say you are having faith that things are as you wish. Clarence Smithson defines faith as "the ability to see the invisible, believe in the incredible, in order to receive what the masses think is impossible".

See the invisible; believe the incredible, which permits you to receive the impossible.

See it. Believe it. Receive it.

If it can happen for one person then it is possible! Do you believe it can be so? Do you see yourself being, doing and having what you want? What do you see yourself as?

This is your time.

What if you could...?

What if this works?

People succeed because they believe, especially in themselves; they listen to as much supportive information as they can. You are entering a new world and you need a guide. It is time to get new teachers. Your teachers show up in a variety of ways. Here are a few ways to find a teacher. You may hear about someone as you are searching for new things on the Internet, from the new people you are meeting and being around, as recommendations from people you admire, and from listening to new tele-seminars and webinars online. As you expose yourself to new ideas and groups you find people who are saying things that resonate with you. Explore what those people are doing. Who are they learning from? Take free tele-classes online. Consider getting a coach to help you get started

Be enthusiastic about the new life you are creating. Enthusiasm is being in tune with that which is the higher side of you. BE enthused! If this all seems too much for you then put it into blocks of time. Give it 30 days. That's just 30 days to having a life that is so much more abundant than the one you have right now. How does that sound? 30 days from today you can be well on your way to living your dream life! Start some new habits and do them EVERY DAY for 30 days and you have cemented the new habits into your life. Or, 30 days from today, you could still be in a less than positive vibration and 30 days older.

Reality is an illusion. It changes constantly through your

unique perspective. When more than one person is looking at the same thing, they are each seeing it differently. The reality you see now is only true NOW! When you change your mind in any way, this reality that you are seeing is gone! To be replaced by your current thinking. So, the past is what it is. Accept it and move on. Look forward. Take the brakes off. Look for the good now. Move forward. The more good you look for the more you are going to find. And then, you can harvest the good.

The big secret to making this all work is...FEEL IT.

Chapter Ten Summary

- A belief sets up a vibration through your thoughts, attitudes and emotions that are matched by the Law of Attraction

- Your mind is your most incredible tool. It takes anything you give it and attract its like vibration to you!

- See the invisible; believe the incredible, which permits you to receive the impossible.

- See it. Believe it. Receive it.

- It is time to get new teachers.

- Put it into blocks of time. Give it 30 days.

- Reality is an illusion. It changes constantly through your unique perspective.

- The reality you see now is only true NOW! When you change your mind in any way, this reality that you are seeing is gone!

- The more good you look for the more you are going to find.

CHAPTER ELEVEN

TAUGHT/NEW THOUGHT

What things did your parents say that are still limiting you?

What I was taught...	My new thought...
Example: There is never enough	I am always provided for.

If I believe I can be a millionaire but I'm feeling like I do not have enough money, then I would be placing my positive thoughts against my old habitual thinking from the teachings I have received. Most importantly, what you <u>feel</u> is dominant! When you give your attention to things that are not in vibrational harmony with your highest and best self, it does not feel good. You are, in that moment, out of alignment with your best self. You can feel the difference. If you keep your attention there you continue to not feel good. Because that's where your thoughts are! The minute you start to think about what you don't want you are going down the rabbit hole. That's why it is so important to recognize your feelings. When you recognize that you do not feel good, then that is when you consciously change your mind and think of something better. You know you are successful when you are feeling good once again. Put your focus on what you want. You deserve all good. Tell yourself,

"I deserve to have the things I desire because..."

_____

_____

_____

_____

_____

_____

_____

_____

Integrating belief and behavior is the recipe for manifesting quickly. So, believe it happens and act as if it is already so. You must believe it for it to manifest. Your unconscious knows! You are connecting with yourself on a whole new level. You have to let go of old teachings that no longer serve you so that whatever you really want can come into your life. By now you should have some ideas on how to be more positive. How can you apply them to your life? How positive are you?

What actions can you take now to be more positive?

_____

_____

_____

_____

_____

_____

_____

_____

_____

_____

_____

_____

_____

List 10 positive words that have meaning for you...

Examples: Happiness, Contentment, Peace

1._____

2._____

3._____

4._____

5._____

6._____

7._____

8._____

9._____

10._____

Now get 10 pieces of paper, any size, and write one positive word on each piece of paper. You now have 10 positive reminders! Take these 10 positive reminders and place them in your environment. See how easy this is?

List 10 results or benefits that you achieve from doing this work...

_____

_____

_____

_____

_____

_____

More results or benefits...

_____

_____

_____

_____

_____

_____

_____

_____

_____

_____

_____

_____

_____

_____

_____

_____

_____

_____

_____

_____

_____

Chapter Eleven Summary

- What things did your parents say that are still limiting you?

- You are connecting with yourself on a whole new level.

- You have to let go of old teachings so that whatever you really want can come into your life.

- What actions can you take now to be more positive?

- List 10 positive words... You now have 10 positive reminders!

- List 10 results or benefits that you wish to achieve.

CHAPTER TWELVE

GRATITUDE

What are you grateful for before it manifests?

Use the 10 benefits you just listed and write them again below after the words **'I'm so happy and grateful now that...'** putting your words in present tense (as if you already have them).

Examples:

> now that I have a coach.
>
> now that I am doing what I love.
>
> now that I have written my book.

I am so happy and grateful now that...

_____

_____

I am so happy and grateful now that...

_____

_____

I am so happy and grateful now that...

_____

_____

I am so happy and grateful now that...

_____

_____

I am so happy and grateful now that...

_____

_____

I am so happy and grateful now that...

_____

_____

I am so happy and grateful now that...

_____

_____

I am so happy and grateful now that...

_____

_____

I am so happy and grateful now that...

_____

_____

I am so happy and grateful now that...

_____

_____

I am so happy and grateful now that...

_____

_____

Your mind is the connection between your body and your spirit.

When you are grateful it affects you on all levels, body, mind and spirit.

Let's look at the people in your life. Take a look at the people around you. Everyone in your life is a result of YOU calling them in with your vibration. You may have been attracting by default.

Who are you grateful to have in your life?

_____

_____

_____

_____

_____

_____

_____

_____

_____

_____

_____

_____

_____

_____

_____

_____

_____

What are you grateful for right now?

I am grateful for...

_____

_____

_____

_____

_____

_____

_____

_____

_____

I am grateful for...

_____

_____

_____

_____

_____

_____

_____

_____

_____

_____

Remember the exercise I told you about where anything you say after the words 'I am' becomes a truth? Think about who you want to become and put that after 'I am".

Example: I am a motivational speaker and coach

I am

_____

_____

I am

_____

_____

I am

_____

_____

I am

_____

_____

I am

_____

_____

I am

_____

_____

I am

_____

_____

I am

_____

_____

You have to adjust your life and adjust your time to create your success. Remember, the definition of insanity is doing the same thing over and over expecting to get different results. Go ahead, do things differently, adjust!

You are worth it!

Chapter Twelve Summary

- What are you grateful for before it manifests?
- Who are you grateful to have in your life?
- What are you grateful for right now?
- Adjust your life and adjust your time to create your success.
- You are worth it!

NOTES

CHAPTER THIRTEEN

DESIGN YOUR ULTIMATE LIFE

Having a vision and a mission is important because it communicates your intentions and motivations to create a conscious future. Your mission is what you are about and your vision is what you want to become.

Your vision is your mental picture of the future.
Your mission is your purpose – what you do, who you do it for and why you do what you do.

State your intentions. What is your...

Vision

My vision is

_____

_____

_____

_____

_____

_____

_____

Mission

My mission is

_____

_____

_____

_____

_____

_____

_____

_____

_____

_____

Now state what your values and legacy are. You values are qualities of special worth, ideals that you operate from like integrity, honesty, etc.

Your legacy is your mark that you leave after you are gone, what do you want to leave for your children and the world?

Values

My values are

_____

_____

_____

_____

_____

_____

_____

_____

_____

_____

_____

_____

Legacy

My legacy is

_____

_____

_____

_____

_____

_____

_____

_____

_____

_____

_____

My Goals:

Let's make this easy and create your goals in chunks...

Thirty days

In thirty days...

Examples:

> I have an extra $1,000 in the bank,
> I have created a home-based business,
> I have met_____,
> I have signed up for _____class,
> I have gotten myself a coach, etc.

_____

_____

_____

_____

_____

_____

_____

_____

_____

_____

_____

_____

Ninety days

In ninety days...

_____

_____

_____

_____

_____

_____

_____

_____

One year

In one year...

_____

_____

_____

_____

_____

_____

_____

_____

Declare it.

Every day I...

_____

_____

_____

_____

_____

_____

_____

_____

_____

These are the skills I want to master....

_____

_____

_____

_____

_____

_____

_____

_____

_____

Know thyself. Know your inner environment. What are you thinking? Just *wishing* for a million dollars or anything you desire is not going to do it. You have to give it a lot of attention. Make it your daily focus. Feel it. Use tools. Use your new toolbox.

Here's a fun exercise...

Create a check for whatever amount you like, made out to you. Hold it and see what feelings come up. If something comes up that is going to get in your way, you have to release it so you have the capacity for the money to come into your life. You must have the capacity to believe.

Do you want to know what you believe about money? Look at your money now and what's happening with your money. It says a lot about your current prosperity thinking. Also, some people think they are being positive about money when in reality they are in conflict. They want more money, but they are searching for a solution about paying bills etc. Searching for a solution is the dominant thought so more searching is what you get.

Your dominant vibration must be that you BELIEVE and KNOW the money is coming. It is on its way! You wouldn't call the catalog company every day with the same order, would you? You know it is on its way. Be grateful that it is on the way to you.

As you release those deep, less than positive beliefs you start to adjust your vibration and you become more attractive – you attract the new things you are now vibrating to! And your new positive beliefs start to take root, resulting in healthy relationships, healthy bodies, and healthy bank accounts.

When you walk your talk positively... you are in harmony with your best self.

> *"Change your thoughts and you change your world." ~ Norman Vincent Peale*

It is not changing your mind about life, it's making up your mind. When you understand THIS then you realize a whole new dimension to yourself.

From this point forward, you are taking control – now you own your life.

It's just a shift in consciousness.

Chapter Thirteen Summary

- Your mission is what you are about and your vision is what you want to become.

- You design your ultimate life: State your intentions.

- Create your goals in chunks, 30 days, 90 days, 1 year

- What skills do you want to master?

- Now you own your life. It's just a shift in consciousness.

NOTES

CHAPTER FOURTEEN

COMMITMENT

What are you committed to? Are you willing to commit to having what you want? Create a crystal clear picture of your future and be committed to creating it. Keep improving the image or the vision; through repetition your whole life is going to change. It's important to become emotionally involved in your own story. The more you stay emotionally involved, the quicker your dreams manifest. It's repetition that alters your programming and then it must turn into results.

Get out of your own way. If you are feeling an inability to be grateful then serve others. What can you do to help someone? Introduce them to someone that helps them. Tell them about a service. Give them information. Give with no agenda. When you want to help people a way is shown to you.

In this moment you are in your power.

Practicing gratitude is good for you. Your attitude changes the more grateful you are. Consciously put yourself in a state of gratefulness for everything you have and for everything you know is coming to you. Are you ready to live in that space? Yes, or yes?

Set things in motion. Keep it simple. And see what starts to show up in your experience.

Gather all of your 'tools' for your transformation – your notebooks, signs, photos, CDs, DVDs, research, etc. Use your new tools to get above the static and noise in your environment. Create a vision board and hang it prominently.

Watch your words. Pay attention! Stay aware.

> *"The most powerful energy interrupters are our own limiting stories, limiting beliefs, and limiting perceptions. They govern our experience and ultimately shape the world around us."*
> *~Mark Romero*

You can create your life anew. This is completely possible for every person. You have the freedom, ability and power to change your thoughts. Right now. In this present moment you have the ability to shift and shape your reality. You can transform your life by changing how you think. There's always something you can do. Every day that passes is 24 hours of opportunity you won't have again. Why not put a bit of that time to work for you right now?

Step outside the circle of your former beliefs. Leave behind bitterness, suffering, lack, and self-limitations.

Release yourself. Make a pact right now to become your BEST self.

You are a unique expression of life. You are here to experience your full potential. Use this lens to now look at life through.

This workbook is a vehicle for transformation and positive change. These teachings and lessons have been tremendously helpful to my own life and experience. I hope it has taught you how to create whatever you want to manifest in your life.

You've got to have it if you're going to give it.

The Law of Attraction

is at the heart of everything.

Chapter Fourteen Summary

- Create a crystal clear picture of your future and be committed to manifesting it

- It's repetition that alters your programming and then it must turn into results.

- If you are feeling an inability to be grateful then serve others.

- Your attitude changes the more grateful you are.

- Set things in motion. And see what starts to show up in your experience.

- Use your new tools

- Watch your words.

- Pay attention! Stay aware.

- You can create your life anew. This is completely possible for every person.

- You can transform your life by changing how you think.

- Make a pact right now to become your BEST self.

- This workbook is a vehicle for transformation and positive change.

- The Law of Attraction is at the heart of everything.

RESOURCES

Online Positive Groups

Join a positive community...Join the Tribe!

Raising the positive vibrations on the planet.

We are a cooperative mindset of positive people and this is a place to help you be, and stay, in a positive state of mind until it becomes automatic.

www.PositiveTribe.com

www.Facebook.com/PositiveTribe

Laughter Yoga - find a group or create one

www.LaughterYoga.org

Prosperity Thinking

www.WomensProsperityNetwork.com

Color Me Positive Coloring Book

is a collection of coloring pages around positive messages. As you are coloring, your subconscious is taking in the positive message and in turn you may experience a more positive attitude. Coloring gently helps you to de-stress from the day and allows you to release negative thoughts by focusing your mind on the present moment.

Featuring:

- A variety of coloring designs with positive messages meant to evoke peace and positivity.

- Images are on one side only to protect the designs under it and to be able to remove your beautifully colored positive message and frame it.

- Simple to complex designs for your every mood.

Available on Amazon.com

Made in the USA
Middletown, DE
13 April 2016